SAY...
Something!

> The Adventure
> of Finding
> the Right Words
> to Express
> Your Desires,
> Reduce Drama,
> and Create
> Connection

MARLETA BLACK

TWO PENNY
PUBLISHING

Two Penny Publishing
850 E. Lime Street #266
Tarpon Springs, Florida 34688
TwoPennyPublishing.com
info@TwoPennyPublishing.com

For permission requests and ordering information, email:
hello@marletablackcoaching.com

Library of Congress Control Number: 2021919482

Paperback: 978-1-950995-52-3
eBook also available

FIRST EDITION

For information about this author, to book event appearance, or media interview, please contact the author representative at: info@twopennypublishing.com

Endorsements for
SAY... Something!

SAY... Something! is a toolbox and the project is you.

This is a book to be taken seriously. Too often we settle for the status quo, telling ourselves "That's how it's always been" or "I can continue to deal with things the way they are." This book teaches us to take control of our own lives. Painstaking efforts were made to bring us gems from some of the masters in relationship and communication as well as real examples from real relationship coaching. But the analogy of how people prepare for an adventure really brought it home for me. We are all so different. Our best tool for communication through those differences... "words," can also be used as a weapon, often unintentionally. Marleta beautifully expresses how word choice can change the trajectory of our lives and daily efforts to connect. She teaches us a new vocabulary, how to speak in a way that brings us closeness and understanding with the people in our life. This book is best read with a notepad next to you or at least a highlighter. These lessons will stay with you long after the book is closed. As they should. This is your life.

Rick Incorvia

Best Selling Author

In my experience, much of the conflict between people, no matter what their relationship, is due to misunderstandings that were never questioned or clarified. SAY... Something! is a deeply thoughtful and practical aid for expressing yourself assertively, exploring your assumptions, and stating your intentions and desires as you live and work with others. I highly recommend it as a tool for personal reflection and taking action to enhance your communication skills and deepen your connections.

Dr. Ivan Misner
Founder of BNI and NY Times Bestselling Author

SAY... Something! by Marleta Black is a wonderful compendium of life lessons in the vein of Conversations with God. Marleta brings a deeply authentic voice to the business of living your best life. She shares her own learning, and her observations of others, with clarity, compassion, warmth and beauty. At times her prose is almost poetic in its simplicity and heartfelt sincerity. Each short chapter provides insight into an area of potential struggle in our lives and offers a simple, doable and helpful reflection and/or action to take to begin addressing each struggle. SAY... Something! provides a generous roadmap to help you choose your best path towards a life of greater satisfaction, happiness and fulfillment. See it as an introduction to, and a pathway towards, your higher self.

Trish Purnell-Webb
Clinical Psychologist, Certified Gottman Marital Therapist, International Author of "365 Simple Ideas to Improve Your Relationship"

Client Testimonials
for Marleta Black

Marleta came highly recommended to me a few years ago from a good friend. My then boyfriend, now husband and I were having problems seeing eye to eye in our on-again-off-again relationship. After having several joint and individual sessions with Marleta, things definitely improved. Her no-nonsense, easy-to-comprehend approach made all the difference in our relationship. (The unfortunate part is that we don't get to see her anymore!) I have referred another couple to Marleta and they had success as well. Two thumbs up to Marleta!

Ben & Kelly

My husband and I met Marleta during the dating stage of our relationship. We had a lot of love and good intentions but a seemingly impossible set of circumstances prevented us from building the family we desired. Marleta never told us how to overcome the obstacles we faced; instead she guided us on a journey to understand ourselves, and how to express our needs and desires to each other. From that wisdom, we were able to define our own path together. We still have obstacles but I feel confident in tackling them with my husband because of the tools Marleta gave us.

Greg & Jess

Marleta was truly a blessing for my family. We were facing some extremely tough decisions and challenges as a family and she was not only able to help guide me with a step-by-step process that got to the core of the issues we were facing but she also helped provide resolutions and execution; with that we were able to bring my teenage runaway daughter home. Furthermore Marleta helped me personally develop the courage and confidence to end an unhealthy relationship and realize I was worthy and valuable. She was truly my angel in disguise and I have referred several people to her that she has helped in the same manner! Thank you Marleta!

T

I've known Marleta for some time now and I really appreciate her candor. She has a unique ability to listen and figure out the deep causes of your concerns, issues and problems. I've watched her help several people around me including my sister and myself. Her training and unique skill set have set her apart from others who might do similar work. She continues to amaze me and I will continue to refer those I love to her.

Dr. Albert Gadomski

CONTENTS

Section One
EXPECTATIONS FOR THE ADVENTURE

Section Two
PACKING LIST FOR THE ADVENTURE

Section Three
FOUNDATIONS, POTHOLES, ROAD SIGNS
AND ROADBLOCKS

Section Four
SURVIVAL SKILLS AND CHOSEN PATHWAYS

Section Five
FIRST AID KITS AND OTHER HELPFUL TOOLS

Section Six
WHEN NOTHING IS WORKING

Section Seven
BEYOND HINDSIGHT

To _____

From _____

Date _____

FOREWORD

On 17 September 2020, I had my first conversation with Marleta Black—and during that initial interaction, I had such a strong feeling that she was a uniquely special human being. Hindsight has proven that feeling accurate. During that conversation, I asked Marleta "What's the big unfulfilled desire in your heart?" Her answer was "I want to write a book—I have a book in me, and I'd like to help millions." Having read this book, I truly believe it has the potential to do exactly that.

What you have your hands on here is a magical piece of literature, which has been written eloquently and with such a thoughtful and careful use of words. The way Marleta has tied her philosophy and teachings together, to take you metaphorically on what she calls an adventure, is genius. This is a journey—which will lead you to better communication in your personal and professional relationships, and which will result in more harmony in your life.

What qualifies Marleta to take us on this journey? She is not only a communication and relationship coach, but she is also an experienced Psychologist. Having now become colleagues and friends with Marleta, I can tell you she practices what she preaches. When we decided to do a webinar series together, she made sure expectations were clear from the get-go. In addition, when she is not happy about something she will tell you in an assertive, direct and honest way, which is impressive in its delivery because it is done in a calm loving manner.

Say Something! is a practical guide on how to become more efficient at conflict resolution, and at times, you will feel like you are sitting on a chair opposite Marleta. Because this book is so absorbing, it's easy to just intellectualize and theorize the ideas taught—fortunately Marleta has given you an action step in each chapter so that you can practically incorporate each lesson. Through these pages you are about to be introduced to a very smart woman, whose true desire is to help you. Personally, I am excited to know I have such a wonderful new tool to utilize for my own future adventures.

Enjoy the adventure!

Lee Roebeck

Mindset & Abundance Coach, Built To Win Academy

INTRODUCTION

Where are you on your life adventure map? If you're holding this book, you've probably struggled in some way to say something, to express yourself assertively, to choose the right words to ask for what you need or want. Maybe you're at the start of a new relationship, and you want to prepare yourself for your new adventure! Perhaps you're 30+ years in, and you are lost in the woods, trying to navigate to a clearing where you can set up a nice campfire and enjoy the peace of your surroundings. Maybe you're single, with no pressing desire to take part in a romantic relationship—but you also know that there are ways you could learn to communicate better with family members, co-workers, and friends. Either way, I have been exactly where you are. I am still you, in some situations. I get it. Learning how to communicate effectively has become my passion, largely because I struggled to do so in early life. Now, having found the voice I have today, I want to share what I've learned so far. I want you to think more purposefully about communication and the power of words.

The right words at the right time can be the keys to unlock the treasures that await you on your adventure. My wish is to spend a few moments of your life with you; sharing a leg of your journey.

If you're like me, you're always wishing and striving to say things better; restate your words more clearly. More than anything, you want to make yourself more clearly understood by others without the confusion and inefficiency of misunderstandings. Maybe you're motivated by peace and quiet. If so, that's enough to keep reading! No matter which of these situations you identify with, I'm glad you're here. Perhaps you're here because someone has told you that you need help with communication. Or, you may be here because there is someone in your life who struggles with communicating effectively. I have a secret for you; we all do.

This book isn't the answer to every communication problem. It is a self-expression of the knowledge I've gained over time while communicating or working with members of my family, work teams, and coaching and counseling clients. I've walked alongside others in hundreds of conversations, seeking better words like nuggets of gold. I'm excited to put what I've learned into the words of this book. I hope those words will reach many more than I could reach one conversation at a time. My heart's intention is for you to read and apply these tips in very practical ways to your life and journey.

I've created this in a brief chapter format for two reasons. First, I am painfully aware of the shortened attention spans we have all developed in this fast-paced world. There is only so much input we can take in, and only so many moments of our day we can give quality attention to or ponder anything deeply. We have millions of options at our fingertips begging for our focus. Secondly, I want you to interact with each section of this book. There are blank lines at the end of each chapter so you can make notes in response to the Reflection/Action section. If you are not inclined to write directly in this book, I recommend you buy a journal to record your thoughts and feelings and planned actions. Blank pages are all it needs; and I will guide you with ideas on how to make the most of it. You will gain more from this book if you take steps to interact with the things you learn.

If you're not the writing kind, please continue to read and think about what you're reading. Let the words sink down to your toes and take root. I know I'm not really beside you as you read, but I will be with you in spirit as you participate. My desire is to help you develop your voice. A voice as important as all other voices. A voice that was given to you so you could "Say Something" and discover the peace that comes from saying what you need to say and helping others to do the same. It takes bravery.

Are you ready for your adventure?

_____

_____

_____

_____

_____

_____

_____

_____

_____

_____

_____

SAY ... Something!

EXPECTATIONS FOR THE ADVENTURE

What You Should Know Before You Go

I hope you see things that startle you.
I hope you feel things you never felt before.
I hope you meet people with
a different point of view.
I hope you live a life you're proud of.
If you find that you're not, I
hope you have the strength
to start all over again.

The Curious Case of Benjamin Button
(Fincher, 2008)

SAY ... Something!

CHAPTER ONE

We All Have Good Intentions

We all have the best intentions. Or, at least we think we do. We all do our best with what we know and what we understand. When we set off on our adventures, we expect the best, most exhilarating experiences, packed with memories and feelings of elation and achievement.

It's important to take that paradigm into every scenario of communication struggle you encounter. If you do, you won't waste as much time wondering about the intentions of others nor defending your own. Of course, there are scenarios where some don't have good intentions, and we'll talk about that a bit later in the book. Generally, we all wake up wanting peace, harmony, joy, love, and positive communion with others. Some of us use more words than others. On the other end of the spectrum, some wish for mutual telepathic silence to achieve their goal. Usually, opposites attract, and this can bring challenges.

This won't be the last time I mention it, but our mistake is to try to make others fit our paradigm or mold. In my relationship coaching work, whether it be partners in marriage and life or soon-to-be-empty-nester parents with their young adult children, the expectation always seems to be the same. "Read my mind, and do as I say (or do) without any curiosity on my part to understand your position." We do this because, as individuals we're most comfortable with ourselves and how we see ourselves. It is uncomfortable to crawl inside another person's skin and feel what they feel, understand what they understand, know what they know. Yet, we must try if we want to have partners in our adventure. Otherwise, you may as well find a good monastery to live out the rest of your days.

We want partners so that when we reach certain summits, we can experience joy together. Likewise, when we're in the valleys, we desire the comfort of someone there with us, knowing we can eventually leave the valley together. Our dilemma comes when we want peace and understanding, yet remain unchanged because we are unwilling to do the work.

REFLECTION/ACTION

Write down the good intentions you have for your relationships. Identify each relationship separately, if needed, as they may differ from one another. Think of your intentions in terms of core values or positively-stated desired outcomes and feelings. Examples of simple core values might be "honesty," "peace," "having fun," or "quality time." Then write down the positive intentions you believe others in those relationships have. This is an intentional exercise where you explore what you want and what those around you want, while rejecting the temptation to note down your mutual criticisms of each other. Those criticisms are always on the tip of our tongue, but are rarely productive as a focus.

As you move through your day, focus on whether you are making your positive intentions known as you speak and act. We often think we do or that others should know us well enough by now to understand us without words. The evidence, though, is to the contrary. Often the longer we're in our relationships, the less mindful (conscious) we are about each other's intentions. Mindfully acting to understand intentions in spite of our experience of others is a large component of productive, peaceful communication. Understanding this will be vital if you want to benefit from this book. Without the mystery of intention gone wrong, there would be no point in trying harder. But we must, so we can grow.

_____

_____

_____

_____

SAY ... Something!

CHAPTER TWO

What Do You Want?

You need to know your destination. The adventure will tire us quickly if everyone involved is not headed in the same direction. In the well-known clip from the movie, *The Notebook* (Cassavetes, 2004), there is a make-or-break scene where Noah and Allie are fighting over what and who Allie wants in her future. The scene is an obvious example of high conflict. Allie wants the best of both worlds; security with her fiance Lon, the young man her family wants for her, and passion with Noah. The beauty of this scene is that both Allie and Noah call each other out on their mixed messages and conflicted decision making. Somehow, they recognize the unfair fighting and are both desperate for the other to help them out of the conflict. Noah pleads with Allie to state her vision for her life, asking her over and over again, "What do you want?" After some intense interchanges, she leaves in frustration, tempting the viewer to think the conflict was for naught. If you know the story, you know that was the moment when the seeds of vision were firmly planted and began to grow into a choice Allie ultimately made in their mutual favor.

Just as those in this scene, we must have a vision for our lives. We must know what we want. And, if we know what we want, we must develop the skill of articulating this vision to someone else. In the heat of the conflict, Allie yells, "It's not that simple!" She's right; it's not simple. But, connecting words to the cloud of feelings in our heads will make the adventure easier. Relationships are a series of moments where we individually identify what we want, then share it with others to see what portion of it is also in their vision. No one ever said your visions have to be 100% compatible; but they should be somewhat compatible. If your visions are only 10% compatible, there will be more painful moments than joyful ones.

We rarely ask ourselves what we want, and when we do, we often don't ask in enough detail, describing 'what it looks like,' much less share it with someone else. It's much easier to say what we don't want, than it is to say what we do. Some of the reasons we don't ask and share are:

1. We truly don't know what 'it' is.
2. Because we're afraid we don't deserve 'it.'
3. We're afraid 'they' can't or won't provide 'it.'

Sometimes we do ask ourselves and those around us what we want out of life, but the questions we use aren't questions that seek new knowledge. In other words, we don't

SAY ... Something!

ask for the purpose of obtaining new, previously unknown information that might challenge our assumptions. Instead, we ask questions having already identified what we want to hear, hoping the other person will offer it up and articulate it for us, so we don't have to. This, my friends, is a waste of energy and is taking the long way home. You owe it to yourself to be the leader, choose the words, and say them. Words are required for true ownership of desire, intention, and choices that lead to satisfaction. Nodding of the head or silence is not true consent. The audible voice must be used and heard.

REFLECTION/ACTION

Take time to write down some things you've always wanted. This is not a selfish act. You were given imagination and the gift of conscious thought, which are tools to envision life to the fullest. Your Creator's vision for you is that you live with purpose, vision, and fulfillment in all your relationships.

Sometime this week, sit down with someone whom you regularly communicate with and ask them some information-seeking, open-ended questions about what they want from life. Start with safe topics about each other's environmental surroundings at first. These can be questions like "What does your dream home look like?" or, "What would you do on your perfect day off?" Then, progress toward bigger topics. Continue on to a vision of how you'd like to give back to the world around you; separately and together.

SAY ... Something!

CHAPTER THREE

Love Doesn't Make It Easier

"Love is at the root of everything,
love or the lack of it."
- Fred Rogers

Love is not enough, even though it is at the root of everything. You may enjoy taking long walks together on the beach or brief moments of romantic bliss, but life-long relationships require more in-depth preparation. Love without the work of discovering ourselves and each other's deepest desires and intentions is not enough. What we often do is make allowances for our lack of fulfillment or for another's unwanted behavior by saying, "But, it's okay, because I know they love me." This may be true. They probably do. You might love them just as much. However, love that isn't willing to change behavior, to express itself clearly, to take ownership of actions and desires, and to confront what should be confronted, is only an academic love. Love is active. Love makes choices. Love says "yes," "no," or "Tell me more about that. Help me understand." Love does not indulge itself in staying passive, or worse, being passive-aggressive or withholding.

Even more challenging at times is the reality that love often brings passion and drama with it. We often gravitate to others who exhibit the same characteristics as members of our family of origin. Likewise, they can exhibit characteristics completely different from, or altogether absent in our family. Either way, drama is a constant temptation. Because our boundaries can be weakened or blurred by love, and because of the familiarity that grows in daily life, drama has a way of creeping in, just as passivity does.

The answer to both drama and passivity is choosing words to:

- Stop your negative assumptions.
- Ask more curious questions to get new information.
- Ask how the newly-learned information can be applied.
- Apply what you have learned through intentional action.
- Ask for feedback on its effectiveness.

Love is reciprocal leadership with an "everyone wins" mindset. The leadership you seek from others is more readily offered to you when demonstrated by you in various ways. Love is not transactional, yet we continuously try to make it so.

REFLECTION/ACTION

Think of a way you may be contributing to the dysfunction of your current relationship or interpersonal interactions by choosing to let yourself, or the other person, get by with unhelpful behaviors in the name of love. Then, challenge yourself to think of why you follow this pattern. Where did you learn to do this? Modeled behavior is a very strong and determined influence. When you learned it, did you consciously decide to follow the pattern? Or has it crept up on you over the years based on historical subconscious emotions that have been buried deep for some time?

Identify one behavior you wish you could eradicate from your wheelhouse. Simple examples might be: avoiding eye contact when someone is talking to you, or replying with, "uh-huh" to everything they say. Ask yourself what you could do instead that would demonstrate a more active love and real engagement with others. Share your experience of identifying this behavior and making the active change. Remember, you're not doing this to ask for something in return, but to simply share, model, and lead.

_____

_____

_____

SAY ... Something!

CHAPTER FOUR

Growth Is Why We're Here

Do you want to experience joy on your journey? If your answer is yes (and I hope it is), you must take steps toward continual growth. If you aim simply for 'steps' on your pedometer (i.e., claiming a certain number of years in a relationship) and miss the opportunity for growth, you will miss the joy. I often speak with clients about life's purpose. "What is my purpose?" "I don't know why I'm here," and "I've lost my purpose," are all common statements when someone seeks advice and guidance from a professional. I typically answer these questions with a statement about growth. We, like the Universe, are here to grow. Just as it expands, so must we. We are here to grow in every way, but one of the most important ways is in the skillful use of the articulated word. Our words solidify our thoughts, give birth to choice, and are at the very core of the lives we create. We are also here to grow while being in relationships with others. Even if you're single and never become a partner or a parent, you need a social network of support. Social support is one of the most important predictors of satisfaction and length of life.

It is tempting to rest on our past growth spurts, circling back to previously traveled paths. We relay stories of glory days when we conquered a challenge or survived an event victoriously. Of course, it is important to recognize those moments of conquering and surviving—but my question is, *What is the next phase of your growth? What is next for you?* When you get in the habit of asking yourself what is next for your own growth, you will be less likely to focus on the lack of growth in others. Projection of your lack of growth will inevitably bleed out onto others, bringing with it criticism, contempt, and a general funky feeling of dissatisfaction. That is exactly what you must guard against. When your attitude is focused on fixing someone else, eradicating their errors, deconstructing their faults and dysfunctional patterns, you become lost on the trail of their adventure. No one wants to take a long hike, much less a lifelong adventure, with someone who is focused solely on finding what's wrong with them while ignoring their own need to grow, reach, and develop.

We all need to find the creative power that we were bestowed with by our Creator—to apply conscious thought to the intention and feeling of a desired state. When we connect this creative power to a purpose outside ourselves, we inevitably lead ourselves in continuous self-improvement and self-actualization. And, we attract fellow adventure seekers who also desire growth.

REFLECTION/ACTION

When did you last grow? Write down a moment in your life when you can remember truly growing in maturity, awareness, skill, or clarity of thought. What were the catalysts of this growth? If the catalysts were sudden or traumatic events, who helped you through them? How did that help result in the growth you experienced? If the catalysts were inspiration, joy, or mentoring from another, what were the specifics that inspired you to grow?

What can you do now to create an atmosphere of growth in your world today? Sit down with someone you're close to and discuss your desire to move forward into new growth. Ask them to ask you questions about what that looks like for you. In doing this, don't frustrate them with reasons why following through with growth will be hard or impossible. Focus on finding solutions. Ask for their support and help. Make this a partnership and make agreements about ways they can help you stay accountable on your growth adventure. The support you ask for can be adjusted along the way, but take the first steps and have the conversation! If it's too confrontational to do this over a formal sit-down meeting, take a walk while you talk instead. In my experience, miracles have happened during one-hour walks. Put your shoes on!

_____

_____

_____

_____

_____

_____

_____

_____

_____

_____

_____

_____

SAY ... Something!

CHAPTER FIVE

We Are All "Difficult" to Someone

There will be times your adventure partner finds you not so adventuresome.

We're all tedious or boring to someone. Yes, even the love of your life at times.

We're all deeply interested in someone else at other times.

We may trigger yet another person to re-experience previously experienced pain.

We all have the potential to use our words for tremendous healing.

The truth is, many of the people we encounter will find us difficult to understand, negotiate with, and accept at face value. Yet, we will likely label them as difficult or challenging— we may even call them 'the problem.' We want to be understood; to not have to negotiate and fight for everything we need, and to be unconditionally accepted as having good intentions. So do they.

Negotiation is just stating what is non-negotiable and what we prefer, one sentence at a time.

What we say to ourselves:

"That (insert annoying person's name here) needs to...

...."Change their attitude!"

...."Get a clue!"

...."Get over themselves!"

...."Communicate!"

Or, we say...

"If I ever told them what I think... It would destroy them... They would hate me..."

We also say:

"No one is listening to me, no matter how many times I say the same thing!"

"You never listen!"

"You're not hearing me!"

"You always dominate the conversation!"

"You always shut me down!"

It's easy to blame and analyze others and run from the mirror when we should look into it more often.

Saying the right words isn't about arming yourself with words that will help you make your point, win an argument, or put your needs before the needs of others. It is about the dance of communication that requires, above all, curiosity.

Never stop asking questions, and help those around you ask more and learn more about you.

"Great," you say. *"I got this book to help me get a word in edgewise with people who are hard to talk to, difficult to live with, and even behave in uncaring ways when I try to get my point across."* While you may discover tools to help in these various scenarios as you read, you may also discover some unhelpful patterns of communication within yourself. Let's not limit your journey to confronting your own personal conversation dominators. We will cover a wide range of communication dynamics and interactions. Through this book, I hope you will gain the courage to try new things that were scary before. You will find you don't die when you become assertive. You begin to live.

REFLECTION/ACTION

Write down the last time you became tongue-tied in a conversation in which you felt shut down by another person. Write down the *who* and *when* of the situation. What was the topic? What was the tone of the other person? What was your tone? When did the conversation escalate? Can you identify what triggered the escalation? Now, write down how you were feeling when the escalation occurred. Did this feeling remind you of anything? Conversations often go south when they remind us of previous situations of restricted expression. Write that down.

As you go about your day, notice the energy you bring to your conversational interactions. When you find yourself approaching a "difficult person," instead of showing them a face that is decidedly not built for poker, smile at them and listen. Really listen. Resist the temptation to surrender your needs before you start, but equally, resist the temptation to be blind to the other's needs. Listen, and notice, and smile, then go write down what you noticed.

_____

_____

_____

_____

_____

_____

_____

_____

CHAPTER SIX

We All Have Triggers

This is the point of no return. The blisters have set in, and all we want to do is take off our shoes, rub our feet, and curse the day we agreed to go on this adventure in the first place. If you've ever taken your shoes off after a few miles, you know that putting them back on is nearly impossible, causing more pain than before you removed them.

We all have those moments when we don't want to take another step in pain. We start to be predictive and assumptive about the behavior of others and stubbornly certain about the fruitlessness of our labor. There are other moments when someone says something to us, and we go from 0 to 100 on the *"What did you just say to me?"* scale! It would be helpful, when this happens, for you to sit down with your journal and identify what happened in your emotional mind to send you to the place where you're blaming someone else for your every blister.

Often we don't deconstruct these moments, their filters, or their triggers. When we refuse to identify what happened and the precise moment things went wrong, we are destined to repeat the scenarios, in some form, over and over again. Even more troubling is the fact that, not only will we repeat it, but we will pick up speed in the repetitive loop, habitually bonding with the words and successive triggers used to push each other's buttons.

It is not only the word patterns we become attached to. The word combinations, together with the rise and fall of emotions, sometimes extreme emotions, are stored deep in our memories. This is often hinged on the history of our "little life," when we didn't have the words to identify our feelings nor ask for what we want, and our role models may not have been the most skilled either.

When clients enact their dramas before me, I often ask them to pay attention to the pattern I am witnessing as I observe them. Of course, this means I need to have witnessed it enough to have seen a repeating pattern. Still, when I do, I'm jointly accountable with them to identify what is happening and ask questions to clarify the pattern's origins and feelings. I may ask, "When in your life has a pattern such as this taken place before?" or "Does this pattern remind you of another scenario or time?" This leads us to the raw emotion and point of vulnerability at the root of the pattern and enables us to identify an alternative thought and behavior, specifically to identify new words that will replace previous words.

When you're a participant in a two-sided button-pushing war (for lack of a better term), you've essentially gone off track, leaving the security of the map. Your adventure is stalled. You're losing daylight, and you may not get to the next base camp with enough time to start a fire and cook your much-deserved meal before retiring beneath the stars. The loss of a few hours turns into a cold, hungry night without adequate rest for the next day. One lost night turns into days of cranky hiking and rationing of supplies. Or worse, not completing the adventure at all.

REFLECTION/ACTION

Write down the details of the last major conflict you had in your relationship. Now write down your best recollection of the script of how it played out, just as if you were writing a movie script. This may seem silly and fruitless at first, but it is a means of processing your viewpoint and reflecting on what aspects prompted the triggered response you experienced. Remember, these exercises are primarily about self-reflection, clarification with your partner, and curiosity about yourself and how you interact with others.

This is not about showing your script to your partner to highlight where they strayed from the map! It's almost certain that they will remember the script differently, so comparing word for word, line by line, may be unproductive. If you're intent on doing this, seek a counselor's help to identify differences in your accounts and bring action-oriented resolution. Getting stuck on the map is not helpful. Instead, take the detail in your reflection and evaluate where you went off the map yourself. Identify where you were triggered and what emotions it inspired. Choose new words to help you remember that there is an alternative route next time. A shortcut, if you will. We often refer to, "as the crow flies" when discussing geography and getting from point A to point B. As you think of that crow flying over rocky terrain, challenge yourself to be like that crow as you move toward conflict resolution more quickly.

_____

_____

_____

_____

_____

_____

_____

SAY ... Something!

CHAPTER SEVEN

We All Hear What
We Want to Hear

We expect people to read our minds, but they cannot.
We actively assume what is on the mind of others as
they communicate.

We expect the benefit of the doubt, but we struggle
to give it.

We expect to be assigned a positive intention, but
we often assign a negative intention.

And, we look for our healing through communication
with others.

How many times have you heard yourself or someone else
say, "You're not HEARING me." It's very common and equally
frustrating. The capacity for each of us to speak without being
understood for substantial amounts of our communicating life
is astounding. We have an uncanny ability to be so close to a
solution at any given point, yet so far away. This is like being
deep in the woods without the ability to see the clearing
just a few feet away. Often our assumptions, combined with

the misuse of our own words, cause us to circle the clearing senselessly for hours.

What we want to say in return is, "No! You're not hearing ME!" Or, "You're not saying anything clearly for me to hear!" Or even worse, we lose a firm hold on our emotions and say, "Spit it out!" If we could wave a magic wand, we might wish people would just say what they mean and be honest and straightforward. It's just not in our nature to be forthright. While it's not in our nature, it is a skill that can be learned.

So, what is the answer to this dilemma? We have to remain curious, to seek more clarity and understanding. We may have to, in the midst of a heated misunderstanding, find the strength to stop and say, "Okay, please help me understand," or "Please tell me what you're trying to say to me." Yes, I know it's the last thing you want to do when you're being accused of not listening. But, do it anyway. No one anywhere, in the history of ever, got offended by being asked a genuinely curious question backed by the energy of an authentic desire for information. They may be offended by their own answer when they hear it, but that should be left for their own reflection.

REFLECTION/ACTION

Write down the last time you were accused of "not hearing" someone, or you felt no matter what you tried, you could not be understood. What was the topic? What was the tone of the other person, and what was your tone? When did things get confusing? Can you identify the moment when the words you or the other person chose became more general and less specific? More flooded with emotion than with clarity? Now, think of a person with whom this never or rarely happens. Why are your interactions with this person different or clearer? Sometimes we can attribute the clarity to our level of affection for a given individual. Our communication components play out differently with that person due to safety, trust, lack of defensiveness, etc. Take a moment to reflect on the most and least confusing communication you've experienced, then break it down.

The next time you have advanced notice of an opportunity to communicate with a person who struggles to hear you or whom you struggle to hear, plan to ask them more curious questions about the message they're trying to convey. It may help to give them two options for expressing clarity, such as, "Are you saying this, or *this*?" They can choose one or the other, or better yet, they can choose neither option and tell you what they really mean. After the interaction, write down what seemed better this time or what clarity was provided because you were brave enough to ask more questions. You may be surprised.

_____

_____

SAY ... Something!

CHAPTER EIGHT

Confirmation Bias Blinds and Binds Us

How foggy are you? When you set out on an adventure, especially the outdoor kind—one of the key components of your success is the weather. More specifically, visibility. Think of confirmation bias as a weather condition that can cause a lack of visibility in your communication and choices. Essentially, confirmation bias is when new information is used to support our existing beliefs or theories. It can also mean we will tend to make new decisions that support our earlier decisions, because not doing so might feel almost like killing off some part of ourselves. Confirmation bias is a bit like fog. And, the thing about fog is, it rolls in slowly. Before you know it, you can't see. This may be a scenario where you need a professional counselor to see through the fog and help challenge your beliefs, or to help apply new evidence in objective ways. Essentially, this is what partnerships in life and marriage are designed to do. When one participant does not see the fog creep up, the relationship is designed to be the safe space in which tougher questions and challenges can be asserted for new awareness and behavioral change. This only works when we continue to foster our relationships and trust the other's input; accepting their influence to bring about change in ourselves.

This foggy condition is not fatal. Patterns of all kinds are generally identifiable and open to interruption and new navigation. Someone has to get the compass out, read it, interpret the data, and lead the way with a new proposed perspective and direction. Again, seek help if this is your experience, and either one of you has stopped trusting input from the other. When you seek help, be open to accepting influence from the third party. Otherwise, you will simply leave more frustrated than you were when you started.

REFLECTION/ACTION

Write down something you believe to be true of another person with whom you share a relationship. An example might be in an area where you observed a choice they made in one circumstance and you've since assumed they would make a similar choice in an unrelated circumstance. This assumption, now adopted as a belief, might be causing conflict or limited vision. Then write down all the reasons this may not be true and explore how you may have misplaced your belief. Older beliefs will take some work—but the key is to play devil's advocate with it; challenge it, argue with it. Write down all the alternative explanations for what you believe to be true in your experience.

Go to your partner or the person who is at the center of your belief and test out your theory. Perhaps you could try saying, "There was a time when I thought [insert belief here] about what I experienced with you. However, I've thought about it, and I think I may have been off track. When I thought about it, I came up with a couple of (or one) alternative explanations. I wonder if you could clarify whether I'm moving toward a better understanding of what happened." Doing this when the person you're communicating with is hungry, tired, or in pain is not a good idea. Approach the conversation by giving them a choice about when to have a conversation. You'll want to introduce the conversation idea in terms of needing a moment to clarify a couple of things, offering up your best effort to understand them better.

_____

_____

_____

_____

_____

SAY ... Something!

CHAPTER NINE

We All Keep Score

"Love is patient and kind. Love is not jealous
or boastful or proud, or rude. It does not
demand its own way. It is not irritable, and
it keeps no record of being wronged. It
does not rejoice about injustice, but rejoices
whenever the truth wins out. Love never
gives up, never loses faith, is always hopeful,
and endures through every circumstance."
(*Holy Bible, New Living Translation*, 1996,
I Cor. 13:4-7)

Thousands of weddings around the world have used this
Bible verse in marriage ceremonies, whether Christian or not.
The reason for this is the profound way it describes the kind
of love, and associated loving behavior, we all seek and aspire
to give. It is this description of love you should keep in mind
as you communicate with others. Whether the communication

is paternal or maternal, romantic or platonic, the presence of this ideal of love will be invaluable.

Our basic human tendency is to keep score and focus our consciousness on what we lack or what has been taken away from us by others. This transactional nature may originate within a given relationship dynamic, but can be carried forward into multiple communication interchanges and with more than one person or relationship. We often expect reciprocal effort from others, even down to the exact last action we took or effort we gave. We think, "I gave, so why don't you?" instead of asking ourselves or the other person what they have the capacity, skill, desire, and intention to give. We should be giving with no expectation of reciprocation.

Transactionalism is the opposite of the adventure you seek. It is the equivalent of hiking in wet clothes, through mud, surrounded by stinging bugs. If you choose to move away from this idea of transactionalism, you could be traveling with a light backpack in moderate weather, wearing comfortable shoes, and enjoying your fellow adventurers on a sunlit path.

The great news is, basic nature or not, we can decide to think differently about our interchanges and relationships. YOU control what you believe about giving and receiving within a relationship. So why wouldn't you reach for a higher ideal to test the theory, especially given that not trying another way means staying in a prison of transactionalism? Just decide to give, and give again.

REFLECTION/ACTION

Think about a relationship where scorekeeping is a way of life. Set aside your memories for a moment and challenge yourself by writing down five ways you could change the game by giving more without keeping score. Release the idea that you will lose in doing this, or that it's not fair to you, or that *they* don't deserve it. Believe that by changing your approach, you will bring about an increase of what is desired by both yourself and the other person.

Now, set a goal to choose two of those actions to put into immediate practice with the other person. Write down your observations each time you have completed the actions. How did your different actions bring about different results? How did you feel about releasing the resentment of past results? What impact did these actions have on your relationship overall or in those moments? If the results were not different, why do you think that was the case?

_____

_____

_____

_____

SAY ... Something!

CHAPTER TEN

We Either Control or Surrender to Our Patterns

What are you surrendering on the altar of fate? What have you given up or given into in the name of a good love story? Are you accepting that average interactions are all we deserve? We can unconsciously become disengaged from the active choices required to achieve effective and enjoyable communication. Such choices are required for rich and fulfilling relationships. Sometimes, this surrender is because we have a paradigm that the other person is unchangeable. Sometimes, we don't want to tempt fate or play God, believing that God or fate may have brought us together in the first place, and so we stop engaging.

Occasionally I find that one member of the relationship knows what buttons to push in order to control the communication dynamics. They do this so communication fits familiar "comfortable" patterns. This is a false comfort. It deceives us on our traveling expedition. We hope for a mountain summit but instead find ourselves in a valley with no destination or vision. Recreating familiar patterns from childhood is a cellular-level, adrenalin-pumping, habit. One that will rob us of growth and enjoyment of life.

Even more complex is the passive-aggressive participant, who has learned to participate through a grenade-throwing type of behavior. They drop a bombshell then run, going straight for the escalation of the other person's feelings. In this way, the instigator temporarily numbs their lack of engagement or unhealthy contribution by inciting the other's overreaction. This is such a waste of energy, yet can become a deeply entrenched pattern over time.

What we all deeply crave is peaceful, assertive, calm, adult-like communication. Yet, if we're honest with ourselves, we sometimes fall into the above patterns out of pure habit. Habits can be changed—thank goodness. Through a conscious intention to make a new pattern, change can happen quite quickly. Yes, it takes two people to make a change. But typically, if one steps forward to lead with loving intention, the other will follow. To risk taking the lead is not a risk at all, except possibly to your ego. The potential gain is far greater than any momentary loss of pride. Increased joy of the journey is priceless and is what we all long for as we seek self-expression and growth in community with others.

REFLECTION/ACTION

Think for a moment about which of the above tendencies you most often act out. Are you the passive surrenderer of voice in the negotiation of life? Or, are you more often the button-pusher? Or, do you sit in the *drop-a grenade-and-run* category? How is your strategy working for you? Here is a better question. What would others with whom you communicate say about how it is working?

Sit down with someone important to you and have a conversation about this chapter. Yes, I'm aware this could get messy. But, life is messy. Communication is complex, and unless you're a genius at it most of the time, it's worth taking a risk to improve it. Ask where they believe you fall in these categories. Be sure to ask for examples, followed by asking how they would like it to be different. Ask them to describe exactly what it looks and sounds like when it is different, word for word. You may be surprised at how well this can be received. Simple changes, once your ego accepts the idea of making them, can revolutionize your communication dynamics. Once you've mastered one change, ask what else you could change. It is a false fear that doing this means you'll be doing all the work. Leading by example will inspire your communication partner to follow suit.

_____

_____

_____

SAY ... Something!

CHAPTER ELEVEN

We Gravitate Toward Independence or Codependence

You think you need me,

but you don't.

You see something present in me that is present in you,

so you're drawn to the likeness.

You see something lacking in me that is lacking in you,

so you're drawn to the deficit

for comfort.

You see something I have that you want,

thinking it will bring you happiness.

It won't.

I am but a distraction to your growth.

Or perhaps, I am a catalyst for it.

In any case, your focus should not be on me but on

who you are to become.

I am willing to reflect that back to you, but I cannot

bring it about without you.

You must be engaged and intentional about it.
Seek it out, but I'm not what you seek.

I wrote this at a time when I realized I was habitually enabling codependent relationships in many areas of my life. Enabling was taking place because I was not using my voice to create boundaries and identify what I needed. It was one of those valleys in my journey I referred to earlier.

Often in communication, we want the other person to be our everything and know what to say without any help—to read our minds. This is unrealistic unless both of you are masters in telepathy and know how to supply someone's everything. I haven't achieved that in life, and I doubt you have either. We want to be known so well that our loved ones can meet our every need and yet we expect them to surprise us from time to time! Not too much to expect, right? Unfortunately, no relationship ever escaped the need for multiple open, rigorous conversations about wants and expectations in order to achieve a long-term, peaceful co-existence. It is simply a necessity that you articulate your needs and wants and not be tempted to believe someone should read your mind or be your everything. If you're walking along the hiking trail and get a rock in your shoe, your hiking partner isn't going to know about it unless you tell them. Why would you expect anything different in a communication relationship?

You're probably thinking, "I told them what I want back on Jan 13th, 2000" or something similar. While that may be true, it's unrealistic to expect that after saying it once, the other person has engraved it into their memory forever. Rest assured, active listening can be learned and practiced. With a solid understanding and intention to show up, both of you can be more present and meet each other's needs more often. Just don't let it stray into scorekeeping or a competition, as mentioned earlier.

Alternatively, you might be one of those people who, at times, expects all the benefits of a relationship without any of the interdependence a relationship offers and requires. Interdependence calls for us to be intentionally giving to each other. Not to outdo, but to give. Not to be codependent and helpless, but to lean on each other in a healthy way. We must acknowledge each other's contribution and be grateful enough to increase our own in fresh and new ways.

I'm 100% certain we all bring our historical stuff into each relationship dynamic. I'm equally certain we can overcome our histories and create something new. We are gifted with vivid imaginations and are made in the image of infinite intelligence. So, our mission is to appeal to our intended design and our desire to grow, developing into willing participants in fulfilling interdependent relationships.

REFLECTION/ACTION

Where are you on this dichotomy of dependence vs. interdependence? Sometimes this is more easily answered in percentage splits to bring it into conscious awareness. Think about this from the perspective of the value you bring to the other person. Now, think of how your current perspective or position influences your communication expectations. Just like when you set out on a hiking or mountain climbing adventure, you need a well-communicated plan for where you're headed. You need to rely on each other for safety and support, while still walking independently on your own legs. Where you come from in your interdependence paradigm most definitely influences where you will end up at the end of a conversation or conflict.

Wherever you are now, write down where you'd like to be. What does it look like to be more interdependent in your relationships? Choose two significant relationships where you'd like to see a shift from codependence or independence to interdependence. What does communication look like between you and the other person across a typical day? Script out that day. Then, write out a gratitude statement that reflects a changed script (new reality) down to the fine details of how your best day of communication ends. A gratitude statement might start with, "I'm so happy and grateful now that..." Once you've developed this new script, begin to speak it, first to yourself, then to those involved in it. As you focus on this, others will begin to engage with you, and naturally follow your lead. Odds are, they want improvement also. In cases where they don't follow your lead, or even refuse to listen, you can seek an outside perspective from a professional, which we will cover again, later in the book.

_____

_____

_____

_____

_____

_____

_____

_____

_____

SAY ... Something!

CHAPTER TWELVE

Effective vs. Efficient

We do what works for us as individuals by default, whether it's seeking pleasure, avoiding pain, expecting telepathic understanding, or some type of compensation for what we didn't get as children. The truth is, what we do for ourselves and our personal notion of efficiency isn't always effective for us collectively in relationship with others. Like it or not, this collective ineffectiveness puts a cyclical drag on our personal efficiency and effectiveness.

If you set out on a wilderness adventure with the best equipment, plenty of protein bars, a good water supply, comfortable clothing, and a good tent, yet your adventure partner came unprepared, this lack of preparedness is now your joint responsibility. There is no such thing as announcing that you will not help your adventure partner in the middle of the forest. The agreement to go on the adventure in the first place requires a commitment to aid the other. A commitment to communicate what is needed when it's needed. A commitment to get to the destination together, with the celebration of milestones and many cozy campfires along the way. At times, this will feel like personal inefficiency, but the goal is mutual effectiveness.

Where are you in your relationship journey? Are you at the idyllic start with all the invincibility that a new relationship brings; or wandering in the desert, not sure how you got there? You might be planning a dream journey with a future wished-for partner. Wherever you are, it is important to believe in your ability to open the map and reorient yourself. Even if it means a little more time is spent at your current base camp. Some of the most ineffective decisions have been made in the middle of the night, hoping that by continuing forward in desperation, a magical clearing will be found by sunrise. Panic doesn't pay. Stop and make a plan. Have a conversation. Reassess the destination. Take stock of the supplies and determine how you'll get to the next safe milestone. Remember, you started on the adventure to have fun! Look up, listen to the birds, breathe in the fresh air, and smile. Your adventure isn't over yet!

REFLECTION/ACTION

Determine whether you spend too much time convincing yourself that the person with you on your communication journey is dragging you down. In my experience, this drag is largely perception. It is usually the result of a lack of conversation and agreement about where you're headed and how you'll get there. Challenge yourself to reassess objectively.

Write down your current life goals. If you're married or in a committed relationship, ask your partner to write theirs down. Odds are you share about 85% of your list and might just be going about achieving them in different ways. The worst that will happen is finding a larger discrepancy than you thought existed, which will allow you the opportunity to come up with a more mutually agreeable set of goals. The remaining 15% of desires are often not life-changers, but if they are, work on them. Discuss them. Rule them out or rule them in.

_____

_____

_____

_____

_____

_____

SAY ... Something!

PACKING LIST FOR THE ADVENTURE

Preparation to Enjoy Your Purpose

———————————

I was amazed that what I needed to survive
could be carried on my back. And most
surprising of all, that I could carry it.

(Strayed, 2012. p. 110)

———————————

CHAPTER THIRTEEN

Check Your 'Comms'

To be heard, understood, and found when you feel lost, you must find and use your voice. Even if you're not in a relationship currently, finding and using your voice is your ticket to the stage on which you can get your message out. In relationships and other human interactions, it's vital to have a voice and agree on which form of communication will be best at which times and in which situations.

The longer the journey, the bigger the adventure, and the more valuable the travel partner, the more having and using your voice is critical. The mistake often made is that we think those we've communicated with the longest, know us best, and therefore need the least amount of preparation, clarification, and attention as we interact with them. The reality is that familiarity and accumulated knowledge about the other person on our journey can actually create such a mountain of assumptions that real communication—the kind we wish for to connect and feed us—gets crowded out by that mountain. I'm here to tell you, every day is a new day. Every day needs a new check-in or several. Decide today that you will stop thinking of your communication as broken or less than. Every new step on the journey should move you away from previous assumptions and prompt you to ask again… and again… *"How can I be there for you when you need me?"* or, *"How will I know you're hurting?"* and, *"How can I tell you when I feel overwhelmed or when I have a need?"* These questions are just as vital to ask yourself so you can minister to your own needs!

In addition to the words used to ask and describe the need, you should also ask which method will be the most effective for each level or type of need. Will you use code words agreed upon earlier, or just say them out loud for others to hear? Will you use a certain look across the room? Will you use instant messaging of some type? Whatever the choice, agree to it early and often. Likewise, agree on what is not acceptable. One example is to avoid using instant messaging or texting for negative communication of any kind. Even when not intended as negative, these messages can often be misinterpreted as negative or devoid of the right feelings attached.

REFLECTION/ACTION

Think back on a time when you got into a disagreement over wishing someone else could read your mind or assess your needs better. You may have felt this simply because they know you or you feel they should know you well enough. Were there ways, in hindsight, that you could have set up some communication strategies beforehand which might have helped you avoid the disagreement? This applies equally to you on your own. How can you be more in tune with your own needs to avoid possible overwhelming feelings of isolation and lack in your world? What are the signs you can look and listen for that indicate clearly the need for you to act or make a change?

Think about the next event or circumstance where you could potentially repeat a past communication mishap. Discuss this with the person you are likely to experience it with. Evaluate it on your own, and then put some safety protocols in place to navigate it. Afterward, evaluate the effectiveness of the new approach. The need to revisit these scenarios continuously is part of a satisfying communication life and does not indicate failure in chemistry, compatibility or functionality.

_____

_____

_____

_____

SAY ... Something!

CHAPTER FOURTEEN

Check Your GPS

Just like the 'comms' referred to in the previous chapter, GPS, which stands for Global Positioning System, is useful for knowing where you are and where you're going. Having a reliable GPS means understanding your adventure map and knowing your desired milestones along the way. If you're traveling with others, it means knowing where they are as well. Do they want to go where you want to go? Have they agreed to the milestones? Did you discuss them before you began? It's not too late.

You must know yourself before you can be someone else's reference point within a relationship. This may mean that you need to do some of your own therapeutic or life coaching work before attempting to fix communication hiccups in a relationship with someone else. At a minimum, it would serve you well to identify your values, beliefs, deal-breaker scenarios, personal strengths, and goals. Of course, you will continue to grow and change—but understanding your baseline is vital.

I see many clients who look to others for validation, clarity, self-esteem, and a reference point for their emotional health. In many cases, they haven't done the work to know themselves well; and over time, as people blend their lives, a true chicken and egg situation can present itself. Questions that come into the therapeutic conversation are: *"Who triggered whom?" "Who started it (the fight)?" "Who gives the most/least generally and during a conflict?"* No one can enter a relationship completely without baggage, but they can seek a more developed language around their past experiences, desired identity, and individual and joint goals.

REFLECTION/ACTION

Starting with yourself, ask, *"Where do I want to go?" "Who do I want to be?" "What are my dreams and goals as an individual?"* Even if you are in a committed relationship, this is worth evaluation and exploration. Write down your biggest goals for your life. Seek out guidance from a coach or counselor if you struggle to put words to what you want. Let your core values and beliefs inform your goals. Explore in writing how others can help you reach your goals. Are you reaching for goals that will help you and others grow? Goals aren't designed to kill time, but for growth. Always for growth. Relationships are designed to amplify individual growth, not be a substitute for it.

SAY ... Something!

CHAPTER FIFTEEN

Check Your Physical Condition

Are you a couch potato? Despite the phone apps that try to convince you that you can go from the couch to running a 5K, going from a life where you're not an experienced communicator or negotiator, into a lifelong relationship will be a big challenge. It may be that assertiveness and connection were not modeled for you in early life, but it's never too late to learn new skills. The good news is, it's easier than you think.

Fitness in communication is all about exercising the win-win muscle. Win-win means that agreements or solutions are mutually beneficial, mutually satisfying (Covey, 2004, p. 103). Without a win-win mindset, you're going to hurt yourself, or worse, hurt someone else. With this mindset, you're going to resolve the majority of issues before they turn into life-changing injuries. Wounds from conflict start like blistered feet but evolve into burning shin splints and torn muscles or tendons.

Deep down, we want winning outcomes for ourselves and others. Let's face it, we all crave the joy of victory and endurance, of saying we did it together, that we outlasted, out hiked, or out climbed those around us to make up for the statistics of failed attempts. Not only that, but having a win-win intention in everyday matters helps us create rapport, find commonality and connection, even if it is functional and temporary, and merely for short-term conversations between work colleagues or strangers in passing.

Wherever there are two or more people with competing methods to get from A to B, there is potential for exercising the win-win muscle. Start seeing these moments as opportunities. If you could overlook the unhelpful method of communication the other person may be using, you might see their desired destination and actually help them get there. If in doing that, you both get to the goal of reaching the destination, you've both won and most importantly, you've lived to journey another day.

REFLECTION/ACTION

Think of a situation, perhaps a perpetual area of disagreement, where you are convinced you always lose. We all have situations we've built up in our minds that are seemingly insurmountable because someone just *won't listen*. Ask yourself if the method of getting from A to B is the real concern or whether B just is not at all where you want to go. This is an important distinction. We often focus on criticizing the method when we are battling with the destination set by someone else. Because we haven't decided where we want to go, we become editors to someone else's plan.

Decide how, in the above situation, you will move closer to a mutually beneficial solution. Write it down to practice being able to say it out loud. If, up until now, you've been engaged in trench warfare over the issue, it will feel challenging to make the first step. But when you do, the payoffs will be enormous. Now go say it. Start with, *"I was thinking the other day that I'm experiencing a change of heart..."* or *"I want to talk to you about something I've been kind of stubborn about, to let you know my mind is changing."* See, that didn't hurt at all.

SAY … Something!

CHAPTER SIXTEEN

Check Your Attitude

Does your attitude need an alignment? When you're on a hiking adventure, if your body—or more specifically your skeletal frame—is out of alignment, your muscles and feet will pay for it in referred pain. Think of attitude in this same way, as a foundation and compass for the effectiveness of your communication. Earl Nightingale, a personal development author and speaker, described attitude as the most important key to our successes in life, defining it as "the position or bearing as indicating action, feeling, or mood." (Nightingale, 1966, 2018, p. 10-11) He went on to say that our actions, feelings, or moods determine the actions, feelings, or moods of others. Note, he uses the keyword determine.

Another way to think of attitude is to liken it to a good pair of walking shoes or a balanced wheel on a car. Wear bad shoes, and you're going to pay. Drive with a misaligned wheel, and at best, the wheel will wear out, followed by real deterioration of the car and genuine risk to your safety as you drive. Being out of attitude alignment means that you may be allowing your feelings or moods to dominate and keep you off track.

When your thoughts are out of alignment, you are often not focusing on the present moment, thinking instead of a past event or a future worry. On the other hand, you may be living in the present but thinking negatively about something instead of taking affirmative action. When your feelings are out of alignment, you have decided to become emotionally involved in being unproductive, perhaps indulging in a feeling of lack, emptiness or resentment. Understand that this is a decision that can be changed. Your behaviors can be out of alignment when you act on misaligned—or simply undefined—feelings.

REFLECTION/ACTION

If you had to choose an aspect of your attitude that most often gets out of alignment, what would it be? You can identify it, but be sure not to obsess about it or label yourself as broken because of it. That isn't helpful. We all have stories about why we're more vulnerable in one or more areas of attitude, but if the story doesn't move you forward toward changing your habits, it's an unhelpful story. Just notice it. Notice it, and then kick it off your path. You don't need it. It needs you. Its main objective is to stop you or slow you down. Allowing the misalignment is your choice.

Attitude checks are a minute-by-minute responsibility. I wish I could tell you otherwise. It takes only a split second for a negative attitude to take you down a side trail or away from the next milestone on your map. One thing that can be helpful is to think of an actual vertical straight line in front of you as you look ahead in space. When a creepy or negative feeling begins to take over your thinking or behavior, check it, argue with it, and dismiss it immediately. Whatever visual cue or phrase helps you stay aligned, use that. For some, simply saying the word 'stop' or 'focus' to themselves or out loud will do the trick. It's so easy to blame others for our attitude. Just decide it's up to you, because it is. When your attitude is aligned, others will follow your lead and pay more attention to their attitudes.

_____

_____

_____

_____

_____

_____

SAY ... Something!

CHAPTER SEVENTEEN

Check Your Energy

Our warning labels can stop others from engaging with us. For years I considered myself a low-energy person. I told everyone who wanted a relationship with me, no matter what the nature of that relationship, that at some point, I would probably let them down with my low energy. WARNING: ENERGY DISCLAIMER! I've since learned that when I'm enjoying something or someone, my energy is plenty enough for the moment and the journey. I've probably lost opportunities for more enjoyable times with enjoyable people because of my energy label and negative beliefs about my limitations.

It's good to know your limits and to understand what energizes you and what depletes you. It is not helpful to restrict yourself from new experiences and adventure opportunities because of your own energy bias about yourself or others. It's equally as dangerous to see a gregarious, seemingly high-energy person coming down the path and tell yourself that they are too much for you or the moment.

Energy is negotiable. Energy is refillable. It's one of the Universe's infinitely available provisions, yet we get to decide how to manage it. You are responsible for knowing how to tap into that supply and protect the baseline supply that came with your personality and natural physiology. Whether you consider yourself low energy, high energy, or moderate energy, understand that it's your responsibility to know what brings you joy, purpose, connection, and new supplies of that energy as you live out your life. No one can do it for you.

The truth is, we often underestimate what we're capable of, whether in a relationship or on our own. We're often convinced we've found our limit of supply and recognize the impending danger of depletion. Challenge yourself to reverse this thinking.

REFLECTION/ACTION

Sit down and make a list of ten things that bring you energy and ten things that deplete it. It is a focus task, not a supply problem. Take the lists and choose five actions you will take to include energy-generating activities in your daily/weekly life. Now write down five ways you could protect your energy from being depleted by others or situations. Decide to remain open to interacting with people of all levels of energy, knowing you will not lose in doing so.

_____

_____

_____

_____

_____

_____

_____

_____

_____

_____

_____

_____

_____

SAY ... Something!

CHAPTER EIGHTEEN

Check Your Intentions

The first thing I ask clients and those who bring me leadership questions to do is to clarify their intentions for their time with me. It sounds counterintuitive to ask that before hearing all of the details, but it is vital to know before we get lost in the story. Some clients come to me to ask me questions or tell me stories with the pure intention of needing to be told they are right, so they can win. But, winning when someone else has to lose is not as fun as it sounds. You can win, or you can find peace. You can win, or you can experience the companionship of a meaningful relationship. Our real soul-level desire isn't to win, it's to have peace, joy, and connection in our lives.

So often, I find that people in communication with each other—whether the relationship is romantic or platonic—have reduced their communication to what I loosely refer to as "sibling rivalry." They turn their interpersonal interactions over to the known patterns of childhood where they fought with a sister, brother, mom, dad, or whoever filled those primary relationships in their early years. They lack insight into the basic default desire we can sometimes have to overpower or level others and allow it to taint their interactions and attempts to communicate.

The problem with repeated historical communication patterns is that it shuts out new possibilities and wonder. We simply stop asking questions. Curious questions are a key habit in your communication life to help break these repeating patterns. If right now, you take away one social media-worthy postable message, hear this: Curious questions are the key to EVERYTHING. Yes, I said *everything*.

REFLECTION/ACTION

Write down your thoughts about your intentions in your communication interactions. Think of a specific person with whom you interact and have experienced frequent occurrences of not being on the same page. List five intentions you have in your relationship with this person. Now, list five behaviors that you know will demonstrate those intentions in helpful and measurable ways.

There will be times you won't be able to adequately self-reflect about your intentions. Unhelpful patterns from the past can be so embedded in our cellular memory that we have literal blind spots, especially mid-conflict. Reflect on whether you are one who is regularly reminded by others of your tendency to follow habitual patterns of communication.

Do you agree or disagree? Perhaps you are the one telling someone else with whom you communicate of their patterns. If you can't agree which patterns need your focused attention, it might be time to get the help of a professional to identify the patterns they observe as you interact.

SAY ... Something!

CHAPTER NINETEEN

Check Your Expectations

We all have expectations, and we all make excuses for our non-delivery while expecting delivery from others. Are you expecting things you're not asking for, secretly requiring things of others without their knowledge? We can truly expect too much from others, never having asked for specific actions or responses. If I had a dollar for every time I had a client tell me, *"I just wish they would (insert desired behavior here),"* I'd be very wealthy. I always respond, *"Have you ever asked them to do that?"* and the answer is quite often, *"Not exactly"* or *"No, not really."* Sometimes the answer is, *"They wouldn't do it anyway"* or *"I don't think they'd be willing to."* You can guess what their homework assignment is for the next session. I ask them to write out a specific request, as if writing to their intended audience, giving information about the impact to their feelings and the natural consequences if no change occurs.

On the other hand, once you have asked for what you want, are you requiring consistency or loosening the expectations from time to time. We can be so empathetic sometimes that we allow the brokenness of others to be the reason we let them off the hook for consistent delivery. Sometimes we let them off the hook because of guilt we carry from knowing we haven't given our all. Or, perhaps we have a poor self-image because we were told in the past that we are selfish, and we'd do anything to prove otherwise, including letting them out of accountability. Sometimes we let ourselves off the hook because of our perceived brokenness or fixed idea of "That's just who I am. I've always been that way."

Sometimes we have asked and clarified, been very specific, and requested consistency, with no change in sight. Sometimes they have told us with their mouths that they will never change, and yet we still expect change to come. You can ask for professional assistance at this point. And, you may also need to face the fact that desire is missing from one or both of you to meet each other's expectations.

REFLECTION/ACTION

Where are you flexible or inflexible with expectations? Have you asked for what you prefer, desire, require? Have you reflected upon why you want what you want? Is it a noble request? Is it within the capacity of the other to provide it? Focus on an expectation you currently carry in your mind that you feel you have attempted to convey but hasn't come to fruition. Write out a series of statements describing your experience, the emotional impact of that experience, the desired alternative, and the emotion that this would bring. Get in touch with how you are responding and reacting to things not yet asked for. Be honest with yourself about whether you have become passively transactional.

_____

_____

_____

_____

_____

_____

_____

_____

_____

SAY ... Something!

CHAPTER TWENTY

Check Where You Need to Grow

Everyone needs to grow. Everyone desires to grow. Growing can be and is designed to be as natural as a plant giving off new shoots from deep inside its genetic design. For human beings however, growth requires conscious choices daily, when desire and design alone are not enough, and when temptations to stay right here in our existing paradigms and habits are abundant.

Growth requires more observation and curiosity, more action and accountability, and a solution-focused mindset. The things that interfere with growth must be actively reduced or eliminated. Our negative assumptions, unchecked fear, tendency to blame, and over focus on problems, act as logs in a log jam and weeds in our garden. Every goal, whether it be a communication, personal, financial, or career goal, is to help you grow.

We're generally good at identifying where others need to grow. Just ask us… we know. Spend any time with yourself, and you will notice the many judgmental opinions that swim through your head all day related to how others need to grow or improve. Your focus on the need for others to grow, as opposed to your own growth, is a guarantee that you will become increasingly dissatisfied with life. Left unchecked, this can contribute to the end of what might have been a perfectly wonderful relationship. So often, I hear couples say, *"We just grew apart."* This is quite bothersome because when real growth occurs in both parties, the result is joy within and for each other. In reality, one was growing, and the other was not. Or, neither person was growing and there was a drifting from the original intended path. While it is true we may grow at different rates and in spurts, taking turns to leap ahead, this isn't "growing" apart, it's just growing differently.

REFLECTION/ACTION

When was the last time you grew? Was it during a change that you chose or a change that was thrust upon you? If you've experienced both types of growth, which situation did you prefer? If you prefer choosing growth for yourself, reflect on what would most prompt your growth right now and resist the temptation to throw the baby (the relationship) out with the bathwater (your perception of the quality of that relationship) in the process of reflection. Focus on where YOU need to grow.

Set a dream goal. Start with a list of wants, no matter how selfish they sound. Then, turn the wants into a goal and then quadruple it. That last step was just to get you thinking about really setting a BIG goal! Goals you already know how to accomplish won't bring growth, so set a goal that you have no idea how to reach. Now start getting in touch with the feelings you would feel had you already achieved it. Take yourself there in your imagination and start doing the things that an achiever of that goal would do.

_____

_____

_____

_____

_____

_____

_____

_____

SAY ... Something!

CHAPTER TWENTY-ONE

Check Your Flashlight

No one goes on an adventure in the wilderness without taking a flashlight. While it's true you only need light for the next step, without that light, you're at risk of hazards on the trail. Think of the absence of light as a lack of understanding. Think of the lack of understanding as the presence of incorrect assumptions. Assumptions have a tremendous impact on our behavior. If used wisely and with imagination, they can be used for powerfully positive results. But, when they're used from a perspective of misunderstanding, the results can be devastating.

Shining your flashlight on the absence of understanding or the presence of a misunderstanding means two things. First, it means asking more about the situation. Secondly, it means assertively seeking a possible alternative assumption. Unfortunately, many times we don't shine the light, or ask to know more. Most often we don't investigate possible alternative understandings.

Sometimes we accept third-hand information from someone else, and this is a killer. When you listen to a story about anything, ask yourself if it's first-hand information. If it is not, you've already lost at least 60% of the content and 100% of the intention. If you don't return to the source, you'll spend a lot of time and emotion chasing your tail.

There are two ways I see people regularly allowing assumptions to rule their communication from a negative paradigm. The first error we make is in mistaking analysis for criticism. By analysis, I mean the benign comments others sometimes make when giving us unsolicited feedback about our behavior. Keep in mind they may not know how to ask curious questions of us, so their comments arrive as statements resembling criticism instead of statements that simply notice what they experience. Before assuming their comments are criticism, ask yourself if they might just be analysis devoid of curious questions. If you're typically the person offering unsolicited feedback in the form of analysis, challenge yourself to change your approach toward questions seeking confirmation.

The second error can compound the first dramatically, magnifying the darkness. When enough misunderstandings and assumptions start to rule our beliefs about others, those can compound into conspiracy theories. We can convince ourselves that others wake up intending to ruin our day or that they are incapable of change or of understanding us. We can begin to analyze their behavior and classify it as aggressive or unfixable because of its origin. Or, because our past experiences lead us to believe that because their behavior hasn't yet changed, it therefore can't. Once this belief of unchangeability starts to take hold, it magnifies our tolerance of the dark, inspires disengagement and hopelessness, and sets in concrete our inability to challenge our interactions with others.

REFLECTION/ACTION

Are you the analyst or the recipient of analysis in your interactions? If you're the recipient, do you receive it and seek clarification or withdraw and assume you're being criticized? If you're the analyst, are there ways you could make a change toward the active use of questions rather than making unwanted observations?

Write down some examples of how this might be showing up in your conversations. Be honest with yourself. Reflect on your role, and determine whether you're making assumptions about others' actions. If needed, ask yourself how you could take responsibility for changing the unhelpful patterns you currently experience.

_____

_____

SAY ... Something!

CHAPTER TWENTY-TWO

Check Your Engagement

Are you enjoying the journey in your adventure? If you're not, it's time to figure that out; your happiness is no one else's responsibility—it is yours. You are responsible for your level of enjoyment, and enjoyment takes engagement. Engagement is a choice.

Some of the ways we disengage are natural to our personality and personal histories, but all engagement is a choice. You may be someone with a tendency toward all-or-nothing engagement; where you incorrectly assume all things have to go your way or there is nothing in it for you. Or, you may have developed a kind of learned helplessness when it comes to others, tending to take in too much of what they say about you and absorbing it as truth. Both of these behaviors will result in surrendering your voice in your interactions and cause you to shut down when conflict or confusion presents itself.

Sometimes disengagement looks like a helpful activity from our perspective, like choosing to absorb the pain when difficulty arises. We convince ourselves that we're the better person, or a peacemaker, when in fact, we are people pleasing and accepting accountability for others. Let's be honest; it's easier to disengage when things get tough. Many people tend to distract themselves with TV show binges, food, or other problematic and time-wasting activities. It's easier to let someone else drive or navigate our direction and blame them when we arrive at an unpleasant location. When our audible words and actions are farthest from our innermost desires and longings, disengagement has won the battle. It doesn't have to win the war, and no matter where you are in your disengagement, this is reversible.

Sometimes we disengage simply because we don't get the reassurance that all is well from someone else. That is effectively surrendering our navigation system and inspiring more disengagement. Sometimes we become receivers of input (such as funny looks, silences, or even passive small talk), and the input becomes over-personalized and all we begin to expect. Too much input without active participation (verification) and engagement (interaction) is a voiceless hell and no way to live.

REFLECTION/ACTION

How are you surrendering your engagement and your voice? Have you always done this, or is it a learned behavior? Are you increasing your participation in your adventure? Or, were you more engaged at one point, but have been deterred by blisters and sore muscles over time? Maybe you just feel dominated or convinced that you are. Is it time to challenge your thinking and your assumptions?

Ask someone you're close to to give you a rating of 1-5; 1 is very disengaged and 5 is very engaged. Yes, this will take some vulnerability. You will have to listen to their response and ask clarifying questions. You might even have to ask for examples. Ask them if you're someone who can generally accept influence and feedback in their experience. If you hear something you feel defensive about, ask them how you could demonstrate more effectively your willingness to be better.

_____

_____

_____

_____

_____

_____

_____

SAY ... Something!

CHAPTER TWENTY-THREE

Check Your Communication Paradigm

If the previous chapter gave you some challenges, I'm sorry (not really). Remember, you're reading this book in an effort to grow. And, growth often comes with its own challenges. So, because you showed up, I'm showing up with you. I was born being honest and blurting out my opinions, and only withdrawing if I perceived someone couldn't handle my honesty. In my young life, plenty of adults taught me that children shouldn't be so forthcoming. So, I've spent my adult life rediscovering my gift of truth-telling and helping others discover their own ability to tell the truth.

What's your communication paradigm? Are you someone who recognizes any of the following statements?

"I hate confrontation."

"This is how I am, so deal with it."

"I don't give a (bleep) anymore."

"No one ever listens to me," or "You're not hearing me."

"They will never change."

"I'm like my mother/father, so I come by it honestly."

"It was a joke. You should be able to take a joke."

"I don't need to be right, I just need you to be more wrong!"

These are all communication paradigms that serve to bolster our personal power and defensive position, but they do so in an artificial and temporary way. They create barriers, not bridges. They do not encourage growth. They do not foster intimate connection nor effective communication. If you identify with any of these, or you have your own *"I"* or *"me"* statement that disclaims your engagement in healthy communication, there is room for growth.

REFLECTION/ACTION

If you don't identify with any of the above statements, you've got a head start. But you're not getting off that easily. I challenge you to think about what your personal communication paradigm statement would be if you had one. If you don't want to own it, what might others say it would be if you had one?

Identify and write down your communication paradigm. We all have one, so be sure to ask for input if you're struggling to identify it. Some of us have a few to choose from, which we pull out for just the right occasion. Now write down a statement of the opposite truth. As an example, one might write, "I'm so happy and grateful now that I communicate with

curiosity and an open heart." Try to come up with a few
on your own.

_____

_____

_____

_____

_____

_____

_____

_____

_____

_____

SAY ... Something!

CHAPTER TWENTY-FOUR

Check Whether You Feed or Starve a Conflict

Are you adding fuel to the fire? Every adventurer knows that fire is critical to surviving the adventure, especially in the dark of night when it is vital for cooking and warmth. Adventurers also know that an out-of-control fire can turn into a life-threatening situation. After all, a campfire without borders can quickly turn into an uncontrollable forest fire. A good fire requires fuel enough to stay useful and, as the evening closes, involves withdrawal of that same fuel to die its own timely death.

I've always been against avoiding a problem, generally. But, just as with fire, some problems need to be starved of attention and energy. Letting a problem calm itself naturally is often better than overfocusing on it and questioning why it happened. In fact, too much questioning of the "why" behind a problem, can be a form of adding fuel to the fire, or avoiding acceptance. Acceptance is required for a problem to begin to dissipate.

"The secret of success is to focus
all your energy, not on fighting the
old, but on building the new"
- Socrates

Socrates was onto something here. In order to break old paradigms and habits we must build the "new" of what we do want. This is not in our nature. Our nature tells us to fight the old, fight what is, and—especially if we can blame someone else—fight those who represent what it is. Sometimes by focusing our attention on the things we don't want, we actually give them energy and strength and make them last longer. This can happen even if we're actively attempting to build the new.

Our tendency to fuel the fire is very habitual and of human nature, not only in the doing but in the absence of developing behaviors that prompt us to reflect upon our part in it. We can become addicted to the energetic rush of each new burst of fire. We can become entranced by the flames and forget their function and how they should be serving us. However human, we have the capacity to vision something better and choose our way toward it.

REFLECTION/ACTION

Do you escalate or de-escalate drama? Do you fuel the fire in the right way? Do you ask others to help you know what fuels their fire in functional ways? Do you own it when you fuel the fire of conflict in unhealthy ways? The beginning of growth requires being honest about this and setting a vision for a controlled burn.

The next time you experience an out-of-control blaze, sit down and write out a transcript of what occurred. You're not going to share your transcript with anyone. The purpose of this exercise is to evaluate your part in the blaze and where you could have doused the fire with water or simply stopped adding fuel, allowing it to die down naturally. You might be surprised to learn that you may have been blaming someone else for starting the blaze. Alternatively, you may have been blind to how you could have helped it end more quickly.

_____

_____

_____

_____

_____

_____

_____

SAY ... Something!

CHAPTER TWENTY-FIVE

Check the Weather and Your Need to Check the Weather

Are you patient or anxious generally? Do you tend to agree with the saying, "Let it be" or "We need to make sure?" When we set out on an adventure, we usually fall into two categories: those who set aside time to check the weather a week in advance (and sometimes every day), and those who set out knowing that whatever weather comes, they have the equipment to handle it.

Our communication can be approached from these two angles. While the "let-it-be" style can be problematic because of disengagement and poor planning, the "we-need-to-make-sure" approach has its own drawbacks when taken to the extreme. Needing to make sure lends itself to controlling the conversation rather than collaborating. I don't have to tell you that this often doesn't work.

Balance is vital in communication. We need planning and to check expectations along the journey, but we also need moments of surrender and letting things go. Honing in further, no matter how we start the adventure, communication needs to find its own rhythm. It needs time and space for communication to fail, receive correction/feedback, and for new approaches to be tried. Not only does effective communication need time, it also needs the right environment and activities to ensure it is safe and reciprocal. Growth is equally accessible by all when each one does their part and participates.

In communication, wherever you begin, you will have to adjust yourself toward the middle in order to sustain your relationships. No one is asking you to give up your identity or personality. But, communication calls for movement, reciprocity and evolutionary progress toward a middle ground.

REFLECTION/ACTION

At which end of the spectrum do you spend your communication time? It could be that this is not currently an issue for you. If this is the case, reflection is still useful to increase awareness for future interactions. Have there been times when your own "let-it-be" nature has left you unprepared or caused you to miss out on enjoyable experiences? Or, have there been times your more anxious approach has fueled conflict or inspired less engaged communication partners to withdraw from you for peace.

The next time you're feeling a bit stubbornly loyal to one side or the other, ask yourself if it's worth moving toward the middle ground. If you're not a planner, make a plan for your next joint activity. If you're an over-planner or worrier, ask yourself to let it go. Surrender your need to check the weather excessively.

_____

_____

_____

_____

_____

_____

_____

_____

_____

SAY ... Something!

Foundations, Potholes, Road Signs, and Roadblocks

Know The Terrain

Imperfection is the key.
Imperfections make us individuals.
That's what makes us unique.

Bicentennial Man (Columbus, 1999)

SAY ... Something!

CHAPTER TWENTY-SIX

Your Little Life

You can't outrun your childhood, aka "your little life." You can, however, give it a healthier expression or voice. I didn't create the term, but I like referring to childhood as "your little life" because it represents a valid part of our life experience that sets the course of who we are and how we show up as adults. Life doesn't begin at 18, and although we can dismiss our younger years as being inconsequential both logically and emotionally, they are actually the foundation and the rudder with which we navigate our adult interactions and relationships.

Everything you did and did not experience in your little life plays out in your adult interactions. We call ourselves adults based on chronological age. However, we can act much younger and regress to childhood patterns with siblings, parents, extended family, and those we might consider abusers. We often act out the unresolved conflicts and habitual patterns of interaction with those in our lives at that time. Spouses replace sisters, co-workers replace fathers, and so on.

The voice we have as an adult is in part dependent upon the degree to which we developed a voice as a young person. If your life is like mine, you might find that you often cross paths with those who resemble people from your childhood. This is the subconscious mind's way of bringing about opportunities for personal wholeness and growth. We rarely think of these encounters as catalysts for growth, but that's exactly what they can be. We often see them as problematic, making villains of others, when we should really consider these experiences as moments that can help us grow.

Our bodies have memories. This I know. Deep in the subconscious mind, the part of us that grows whatever we plant, or is planted by others, we yearn for our childhood patterns to be repeated and healed. If we were raised with yelling, we tend to yell or want to be yelled at. If we were raised with button-pushing, we push buttons, instigate, or settle to be with those who do. From childhood, we can become addicted to the feelings of fight, flight, frozen numbness, and drama for drama's sake. If we were raised with passive avoidance, we might settle for that, too. Or, we can feel so exhausted from these tendencies that we swing the other way widely, seeking the opposite of our early experience. Either way, confrontation of the patterns in adulthood is unavoidable. The sooner you face this and seek help to address it, the better.

The good news is, with awareness, your habits can change—all of them. Patterns can be identified, interrupted, and replaced with new patterns by conscious choice. This should excite you! It should also tell you that if you're trying to change things with someone who doesn't wish to be aware, grow, and change, you're in for a tough journey.

REFLECTION/ACTION

Do you find yourself repeating patterns of engagement in your adult relationships, or worse, find yourself in a toxic relationship that feels addictive or inescapable to you? Think about what the patterns represent from childhood. This is one area where I highly recommend seeking guidance in the form of therapy to help navigate these repeating patterns. Bringing forward potentially traumatic memories—or, even the realization that you've been a willing participant in more benign patterns from childhood—calls for a compassionate and aware therapist or counselor to help you process what you discover. The goal is not only to process the past, but build what you wish to see in new patterns and habits.

_____

_____

_____

_____

_____

_____

_____

_____

_____

_____

_____

_____

_____

_____

_____

SAY ... Something!

CHAPTER TWENTY-SEVEN

Your Comfort Zone

The people in your life don't wake up every day to make you miserable. *There*, I said it. Stop assuming that the differences and conflicts are intentional, and you'll be more than halfway on your way to the peaceful acceptance of your differences. So much of your daily adventure experience is influenced by what I call your comfort zone. This is how you act when no one else is around, and you're free to choose how you think, feel and behave. Many of us take our comfort zones into relationships expecting others to do as we do, and to be comfortable the way we are comfortable. So many of us observe and label the comfort zones of others as an intentional attack on our comfort. This just isn't true.

A majority of the conflicts or stories of aggravation my clients present to me are about seemingly minor things like loading the dishwasher, or cleaning (or not cleaning) the house. Or, they can be about how things in the home or work environment are arranged or stored. Specifically, conflict can occur over how we approach a given task, sequentially or randomly, with great detail or big picture approaches. Conflict will most always occur over timing. *How late is late? How early is early? When do decisions need to be made? With lots of research, or none at all? With the feelings of people taken into account, or based on fairness and the rules.* Even more conflict can arise over energy and how it is depleted and restored.

Make no mistake, you won't change someone's comfort zone, but you can find compromise through discussion, negotiation, and sometimes just letting things be. In an adventure, some will want to make the plan for the day and map it all out before they go. Others will want to be spontaneous and see what they find. Both are valid ways to venture out.

When I work with conflict, I often first try to identify the comfort zones of every person involved as most conflict originates from this basis. The problem is we tend to make a bigger deal out of the conflict than we need to and it becomes part of our unhelpful story, to prove ourselves right, instead of actively creating space for who they are and how they approach things. We all love a good story, but if the story comes before the relationship, our priorities are wrong.

REFLECTION/ACTION

Think about where you live in your comfort zone. More importantly, think about instances where you have tried to make others fit your way of thinking. Have you spent needless hours battling over insignificant matters when you could have just found a middle ground through simple discussion?

There are several temperament and behavioral style assessments you can undertake to better understand your comfort zones. It is a good idea to seek the help of a licensed practitioner of these assessments to ensure you debrief the results thoroughly and with care. This will help ensure you don't label yourself or others as the at-fault party when you do the assessment work. Remember, there's no wrong or right way to be. There is only potential for negotiation and compromise in all things.

_____

_____

_____

_____

_____

_____

_____

_____

_____

_____

_____

_____

_____

_____

_____

_____

_____

_____

_____

SAY ... Something!

CHAPTER TWENTY-EIGHT

Your Trauma Stories

Some of us have scary stories to tell, and sometimes we want everyone to hear our stories and understand. As mentioned in the previous chapter, stories do inform who we are, but they can be entirely unhelpful when it comes to personal growth. Trauma can play a part in our history, but it isn't the starring role unless we make it so. It isn't the hero— you are. Decide to overcome your past trauma. Decide that it won't define or limit you. What I mean is, the story informs us about the vulnerability we may carry or the trigger we may be susceptible to, but not about the potential to overcome it. We are destined to rise up from our stories!

REFLECTION/ACTION

This reflection is straightforward. If you've been a victim of trauma—which is in the eye of the beholder—don't reflect alone. Don't spend time wondering if it has affected you, because it likely has. While we may believe we can compartmentalize it, that will only be the case for so long, and no one can define for you how long that will be.

I recommend that anybody with past trauma sees a professional to help process their experiences. There are wonderful trauma therapies available today, and you owe it to yourself to seek them out and address what needs to be addressed. I recommend someone who specializes in trauma and who understands the concept of post-traumatic growth, which asserts that trauma can and should lead to meaningful personal growth.

_____

_____

_____

_____

_____

_____

_____

CHAPTER TWENTY-NINE

Your Love Language

Love isn't an equation. It's not an exchange of equivalent effort and behaviors. Each of us has a specific love language that we use to show others our appreciation for them. This language can be high or low in verbal expression. In fact, it can be completely without words. If you've never evaluated your love language, do it! It will change your entire perspective on your relationships at home, at work, and within your extended family. It will help you understand that you don't always get what you give and that you may need to work outside your preferred love language to express love to another, so they can receive what they need.

The best resource for this is Dr. Gary Chapman's book, "The 5 Love Languages: The Secret to Love that Lasts" (Chapman, 2015, pp. 119-130). There is also an online assessment you can take to determine your love languages (https://www.5lovelanguages.com/). When we identify the individual differences between us, life gets less complicated and more clear. Communication becomes easier when we stop approaching each other as adversaries and start thinking about each other as uniquely created beings.

REFLECTION/ACTION

How do you like to be shown love? How do you like to show it? Does what you do to show love go unseen or unappreciated? There may be a valid reason beyond an unwillingness in others to acknowledge it or a perceived unwillingness to give us what we need.

Get the book, take the quiz, and discuss your love language with others, focusing on your first and second preferences. Beyond that, discuss what it would look like to put this into practice. In other words, discuss your unique way to give and receive within your preferred love language. Each of us has our own unique way of expressing love, and it's all valid and right, so discuss the details using lots of examples!

_____

_____

_____

_____

_____

CHAPTER THIRTY

One-Sided Psychological Contracts

Beware of the one-sided psychological contract.
The concept of psychological contracts originated from organizational psychology in an attempt to better understand relationships between employers and employees, but it is equally translatable to relationships of all kinds. (Rousseau, 1995, p. 34).

If you're asking what I'm referring to, think about the expectations you've brought on your journey that have not yet been voiced or met. These unmentioned and unmet expectations are a kind of one-sided psychological contract. When the contract you form in your mind is broken, due to these unmet expectations, part of the heart can break. Disillusionment and disappointment can set in. When this goes unexpressed, we subconsciously tend to become transactional. We want to get even, in whatever way makes sense to us at the time, or whatever way numbs the temporary pain of the disappointment.

Getting even feels good... for a few minutes. After that, we just look for confirmation in the form of the next broken contract. Looking for (expecting) broken promises can become a way of life, a way of communicating. Or rather, a way of not communicating. We participate in a kind of transactional terrorism, where the demands can get stronger as time passes. When we fall into this pattern, we begin to permanently label ourselves as victims of the broken promises and label others as the perpetrators. This can all be avoided with a few conversations aimed at identifying our expectations and requesting a different outcome.

REFLECTION/ACTION

Where has your heart been broken? I'm referring to little chips and cuts from these broken one-sided contracts. This kind of hurt can be shoved aside and minimized until it cannot. Did you address the pain, or absorb it, making a secret deal with yourself that you would eventually even the playing field? How have things changed since you started your adventure? Is it time to bring up uncomfortable topics of conversation and make some requests? Is it time for you to prepare to be confronted in equal or even greater measure? Do you want growth or the status quo? It's time to decide.

Write down some areas where small wins could be negotiated for all involved, resulting in more positive feelings between you and your adventure partner. Begin with behavior-focused areas of conversation so you can easily define what you want. Then move to the attitude changes and new positive assumptions you'd like to see. Small wins lead to larger wins. This leads to reduced transactionalism, which ultimately leads to increased peace.

_____

_____

_____

_____

_____

_____

_____

_____

_____

_____

_____

_____

_____

_____

_____

_____

_____

_____

_____

_____

_____

_____

SAY ... Something!

CHAPTER THIRTY-ONE

Soulmates and Muses

You have more than one soulmate. Movies, romance novels, and the real-life love stories we've been told by the generations that came before us sometimes lead us to believe otherwise. The reality is that every successful relationship takes hard work, negotiation, conversation, action, belief, faith, sheer persistence and tenacity. And, it's entirely possible that you could be successful with more than one unique human being, given the right amount of effort, attention, and intention. Surrendering the idea that there is only one soulmate for you is the first step.

By the same token, this isn't permission to hop from relationship to relationship to find greener grass at every seemingly insurmountable mountain. Some people come into our lives to teach us things, rather than being committed partners in life. It's important to understand the difference. Partners can certainly have soulmate qualities, but life partner relationships also require aspects that balance and complement us in terms of perspective taking and logistical help. They also challenge us to grow and stop wasting our faith on our own self-deceptions and limiting beliefs.

I've encountered several types of muses or teachers throughout life who have been important in my personal development and have blessed me with their presence, but who have not been intended as a life partner. Some teach us devotion, provision, perseverance. Others teach us passion and faith. Some enlighten us in the arts with talk of music and philosophy, while others teach us to stand up for ourselves and our own purpose. Some muses bring us laughs, and some bring us tears. Some bring us a feeling of safety and are a voice of reason and wisdom. Some point us toward God, and some point us away. Some help us appreciate food and the sensory side of life, and others just help us count our blessings, speak appreciation, and smell the roses. Enjoy them all. They're all important for your life's mission which is to grow. They just aren't all potential committed life partners.

REFLECTION/ACTION

Have you ever confused a muse for a potential life partner? What did you enjoy about the person's presence in your life? How can you appreciate their qualities and contribution without allowing them to pull you away from the focus of your committed relationship?

Walk through your past relationships and friendships mentally, and write down the qualities that drew you into each one, no matter what the nature of the relationship. The intention here is to understand what draws you in to others so you can more assertively ask for it to show up in your current relationship. Not all aspects will be able to be brought into the present, but you'd be surprised how much could be woven in if you simply asked for it. If you're single, this is even more important to help you identify what you truly desire in a relationship. If you don't know, you won't ask. And, if you don't ask, you won't get what you want.

_____

_____

_____

_____

_____

_____

_____

SAY ... Something!

CHAPTER THIRTY-TWO

A Word About Sex

Sex is vital. Period. Sexual expression within the safety of a healthy and intimate relationship is the bomb. However, so many miss the fact that sex is never going to be what you see in the movies and other forms of visual media. It's important to remember that these are productions where several directors are involved in coordinating each move and spoken word. Don't let that stop you from pursuing your ideal scenario within your relationship or thinking about and imagining your ideal while you're still single, just understand that your productions will only be directed by you and your partner.

I talk with so many couples who have just resigned themselves to the fact that their partner isn't getting it right or that they are not feeling it anymore. Here's the good news: with the help of a specialized therapist, sex can improve. On the flip side, there might be troubling news for some: sex has to be discussed in order for improvement to happen. Yet, so many of us have shame attached to the topic and the words are stuck in our deepest hiding places. I have a joke I tell clients. If one of you has tastes that involve purple aliens from space and one of you prefers a wider spectrum of activity, you're going to have to talk about it.

We most often feel that we are weird or dirty in our preferences, or that our partners are just not good at it or would judge us for our desires. If we resort to this kind of thinking, we can begin to feel that trying to make things better is useless. Or, worse yet: that our partners should read our minds because they love us. I'm sorry to say that this isn't true. Even if you started life as the most *on fire* couple physically, over the course of time your biology changes, tastes change, aesthetics change, and these all have to be discussed in order to maintain a healthy sex life. I wish it weren't so, but sex and telepathy were never terribly compatible for longer than a few seconds. Get to work discussing this with your partner and get help if you need it!

REFLECTION/ACTION

Have you ever thought about your individual preferences and their origins? Not just for sex but for physical touch of all types. The latter is especially important as it often is the pathway to the former. Think about it. Define it. Imagine it. Understand it. Accept it. As long as it's legal, give yourself permission to own it and ask for it.

Make a list of all the past interactions you've had sexually and what you enjoyed and didn't. Without assigning the preferences to a specific person in your past, get to work discussing your list of preferences with your partner. This list isn't about past persons per se; it's about what drew you to them physically, chemically, and romantically. It may be that you simply want to return to doing things the way they used to be done with your current partner, and somewhere along the road, life stopped you. The good news is perfect practice makes perfect. If you're single, get to work putting words on your wish list. You're going to need the words ready.

_____

_____

_____

_____

_____

_____

_____

_____

_____

_____

_____

_____

_____

_____

_____

_____

_____

_____

_____

SAY ... Something!

Survival Skills and Chosen Pathways

Knowing Your Communication Strategies

Everyone has a part of
themselves they hide. Even from
the people they love most.

The Amazing Spider-Man 2 (Webb, 2014)

SAY ... Something!

CHAPTER THIRTY-THREE

Assertiveness Is the Happiest Road

Why do we make asking for the things we want so hard? We will do almost anything to avoid assertiveness even when we see glimpses of the peace it brings. Strategies in communication generally fall into four broad categories: Passive, Aggressive, Passive Aggressive, and Assertive. My desire is to point you in the direction of Assertive Choices, 100% of the time. Unfortunately, for many reasons, it's unlikely you'll achieve that. Modeling of communication by those who raised us (or did their best to) is the most impactful factor. Involving ourselves in extended relationships and interactions that haven't challenged us to grow or become more assertive is the other main contributor. Neither is a reason to ever give up trying to use your voice to ask for what you want.

Assertiveness means being honest about your feelings, your opinions, or even your rights. Remaining passive in situations that mean a lot to you can result in feelings of being manipulated, used, or disrespected; even when you believe it's what others want. Being assertive is just as important when your feelings are positive as when they are negative. Expressing positive feelings and affirming yourself and others when times are good is powerful and necessary for relationship health.

Ultimately we fall short of assertiveness because we're afraid to feel vulnerable or hurt others. Or, we get some type of reward from the other strategies. Rewards for outbursts of aggressive behavior include quickly getting the other person to move toward what we want. Rewards for passive behavior include temporary moments of false peace and simple avoidance of discomfort.

Practically, assertiveness utilizes "I" statements to express your experience to others so you can either encourage repetition of the desired outcome or encourage change toward the desired outcome. (Bower & Bower, 2004). Your experience is expressed in relaying facts and events, as well as the feelings they inspired so that you can engage others in hearing and caring about the emotional impact in clearer ways. The key to assertive communication is helping others to not only hear you, but to understand how they can improve the situation at hand. But there's more to the assertive approach. If all we do is walk around complaining about events and feelings, no one will want to make a change. We must provide the desired alternative to the experience we're having, and therefore give others a choice to make changes. The key to lasting change is clearly explaining what is being requested followed by describing the natural consequences if no change occurs. If we express this clearly and others decide not to move toward us in solution finding, they are making a choice they have a right to make. As hard as it may be, we should honor the choices of others.

REFLECTION/ACTION

How effective are you at assertiveness? Could you improve? The answer is yes. The remainder of this section gives some definitions of roles we might play or behaviors we tend to exhibit which can stand in the way of assertiveness. The aim isn't to read this and put labels on others with whom you communicate, but to do a little self-reflection on what you might be employing as unhelpful strategies. The bottom line is, once these behaviors have been identified and discussed, they can typically be corrected. Later in this book, we will talk about what to do if the change seems impossible in your situation and you've tried to bring about change without success.

_____

_____

_____

_____

_____

_____

_____

_____

_____

_____

_____

_____

_____

_____

_____

_____

_____

CHAPTER THIRTY-FOUR

Passive Pathways Delay Your Arrival

Sometimes we're too good at rolling with resistance or having a high adaptability skill with difficult people and that can contribute to dysfunction. If you have a tendency toward passivity, you probably pride yourself on the fact that you are putting others first, and putting yourself second (or last). You may even think that this is what makes you a good person, or someone who keeps the peace. Surrender can be a good thing sometimes, but it can quickly become counterproductive if it's your main way of operating. If you lose yourself in passive surrender, it has the potential to be taken for granted and abused if it goes unappreciated or unseen. More importantly, it's a missed opportunity to find your voice and grow.

The following are some examples of passivity. You may recognize yourself in this list, or you may recognize that others you communicate with follow this path. You may have displayed or experienced other types of passivity, but these are the types I encounter most in my coaching. Usually, these behaviors have been modeled by a passive person and set up as an ideal way to keep things balanced, quiet, and safe. These behaviors stand a strong chance of being altered, however, and should be sacrificed in favor of more assertive expression and emotional authenticity.

The Soother - Soothers engage in placating or acting in a way that makes others less angry or hostile. By acting in this manner, they inhibit the potential development of the other person by interfering with or not expecting the expression of authentic feelings.

The Shrinker - This person uses phrases or throw-away lines to minimize or dismiss emotion. They might say things such as, *"It's all good"* or *"You'll be fine,"* which only serve to inflame emotion, despite positive intentions.

The Rabbit Hole Dweller - When things get tough, this person tends to go down the rabbit hole and they don't wish to be found. They avoid, withdraw and disengage. At their core, rabbit hole dwellers are usually uncomfortable with excessive expression of emotion. This tendency can be naturally present in a less verbal temperament and is more pronounced when a parent was overly expressive with emotion at the expense of the feelings of others.

The Dependent Enmesher - Enmeshment describes a relationship between two or more people in which personal boundaries are permeable and unclear. This often happens on an emotional level where two people *feel* each other's emotions, or when emotions rise and fall in tandem with each other in a relationship. Dependent means this has moved to a level where one's ability to act independently (e.g., make decisions, identify feelings that are your own, communicate from your perspective alone) decreases or vanishes altogether. It may mean valuing approval from others more than valuing yourself. It often means protecting the other person more than you care for yourself. This might be best identified as a lack of trust in oneself.

The Hamster - This person is blinded by their own numbed emotions and habitual responses they've begun to employ in communication with others. They are so ingrained in this pattern that they are unable to interrupt the pattern without outside help.

REFLECTION/ACTION

Do you recognize any of these roles? When have you displayed these behaviors? Did you feel as if you had a voice? If not, why?

_____

_____

_____

_____

SAY ... Something!

CHAPTER THIRTY-FIVE

Aggressiveness Takes You Off the Trail

Aggressiveness is just never ever the answer. Ever. Aggression is born from not being understood, heard, or validated in one's little life, and persists through habitual trial-and-error behavior as we move into adulthood. We will continue the pattern of aggression as long as others allow. While we may have valid circumstances for its origins, we have to take responsibility for these habits in order to change. If we have a heart, or practice any type of self-reflection, we regret acts of aggression almost as soon as the words come out of our mouths. Despite this, we often continue on the path until other alternatives are taught, practiced, and transformed into more permanent habits through accountability.

Here are some examples of aggressive behavior. Again, this isn't an exhaustive list but gives you an idea of what it looks like so you can make your own assessment of your behavior and the behavior of those in your communication world.

The Isolator - The isolator simply says, *"You're mine,"* *"You belong to me,"* *"I need to give you permission for where you can go, who you can speak to, and what you can do with your time."* In extreme circumstances, this can develop into physically abusive situations. In most cases, isolators work on the premise that information from disintegrated or separate sources can't be verified and cross-checked. Although we know they can be, they often are not, allowing this behavior to continue. If they become the only source of information or feedback for you or your growth, it's not healthy. Period.

The Instigator - These are the people who say things like, *"I'm just going to put it out there"* before they drop an inflammatory bomb of meanness. They know what upsets you and intentionally push your buttons by bringing things up mid-conflict. Sometimes they just want to start a conflict out of boredom or their own unexpressed pain. If I know it hurts you to tell you you're acting like your mother (who may have been dysfunctional in your world), I certainly know what I'm doing, and no amount of my own pain makes it acceptable for me to do so. If you're living with a button-pusher who is seemingly unaware of their habit and calling it to their attention only further escalates the conflict, you'll need some help from a counselor.

The Grenade Thrower - Throwing a grenade is similar to the actions done by an instigator, but it differs in that it is typically done in front of an audience. It is saying things from pain or bringing up a topic with the intention of embarrassing the intended receiver in front of others in a social setting. This is not okay, to say the least. This is often done because, in the moment, it's safe to throw a grenade and then hide in the safety of a crowd (aka the trenches). The grenade thrower underestimates the confrontation waiting in the next private moment, if the grenade target takes the opportunity later to point out their lack of appreciation for the grenade. In some cases, that is what the grenade thrower is looking to repeat, the recurring private argument that is at least some type of attention, resembling familiar patterns.

The Screaming Yeller - Do you live with, or are you someone with only one tone and volume setting? Screaming Yellers are loud, aggressive, accusatory, and completely disconnected to emotions on the part of anyone involved, including themselves. At some point in their lives, this behavior was modeled by someone in authority. The behavior was historically rewarded and has found a home inside their cellular memories and neural pathways, masquerading as a normal way of being.

REFLECTION/ACTION

Where have you seen these behaviors? What other aggressive behaviors have you exhibited that you would ideally like to eradicate from your repertoire? Think of cycles where you or someone you communicate with has had to apologize repeatedly for the same aggressive behavior with no end to the pattern in sight.

_____

_____

_____

_____

_____

_____

_____

_____

_____

_____

CHAPTER THIRTY-SIX

Passive Aggression Is the Road to Nowhere

Oh, passive aggression… my favorite. I say that this is my favorite because it's the one behavioral pattern that most cries out to have a healthier voice, but has so many shades and side-tracks that were formed to avoid true assertiveness. For these people, assertiveness was never safe in their little life, and so in some ways, their communication needs new parentage. This trait is one of the most intriguing to inquire into and to "course correct." I also find that in doing so, it brings true joy and peace to the person imprisoned by its patterns. Here are a few examples that might seem familiar to you.

The Reinforcer - In an attempt to strengthen their position in a conflict, this person often seeks out one other person for validation, forming a triangle. The person they seek out to form a temporary power alliance is often important and influential to the person with whom they have the original conflict. It's like putting on a suit of armor, knowing the moment you take it off, you're still vulnerable and in deep need of resolving the conflict with the source.

The Scatterer - Scatterers seek out as many people as possible for validation and reinforcement when conflict arises. It starts with one but moves quickly to multiple contacts, and has the functional purpose of making one feel less alone in the fight. This method is passive because it doesn't speak with the source, but is also considered aggressive because it often thrives on the buzz of getting others on their side and proving their point to the person with whom they have the conflict. This is never helpful, and when the buzz wears off they're still alone in the fight. In the worst case, the people they've managed to get on their side may have started a war on their behalf that could run for years, and they'll still be alone in the fight.

The Attention Seeker - Attention Seekers just want to be famous. Famous in a way that they feel publicly seen by authority figures or people who might advance them and their voice in some way. The problem is they haven't done their own work to develop that voice or earn their time in the spotlight. They are seeking a shortcut to the mountaintop. Within a relationship, attention seekers will seek out social circle audiences to get validation. This often manifests through being the life of the party at the expense of the needs of others. It may involve cornering an unsuspecting new person to the circle to win them over before anyone else can. They can also seek attention by participating in dialogue within a partnership in a disingenuous way, as if to prolong the discussion while keeping actual intimacy at bay. This is essentially filling conversations with words that go nowhere. This is a layer just above small talk and talking about the weather. Unintimate, undeep, unfulfilling, and yet it keeps you talking, spending energy, and treading water. If you're partnered with an attention seeker, you will know this well.

The Gonna - This person overpromises and under-delivers. An example might be promising to commit to quality time in the future or go on vacations to make up for their mistakes in the relationship. They're the people who say *"We really should get together,"* but never make the reservation or call to schedule. They're the people who say, *"One day I'll take you to Paris,"* and never make the travel arrangements. Overpromising and under-delivering breaks hearts and should be confronted.

The Scapegoat Finder - Also known as the *Common Enemy Flip.* Through their defensiveness, they work subconsciously or consciously to blame the crime on someone with whom you already have a beef. The healthy alternative is to simply take accountability for their actions, apologize, and question how the circumstance could be avoided in the future. If, however, they can get you lured into discussing the common enemy, they have won the moment, evaded the conflict, and evaded accountability.

The Subject Changer - Subject changers often grew up with a parental figure who modeled this behavior. Just when you confront one of their behaviors, they split off on a side street and bring up something somewhat related but different enough to throw you off. The true experts can subject change several times within a 10-minute argument. What's worse is you can follow them right down the path unless you recognize mid-stride that it is happening. It's rare for you to be able to recognize it while it's happening because it often happens when both parties are in an overwhelmed emotional state, and neither is actively recognizing that the subject is being changed. After so long in this habit, we can give up challenging this behavior—especially when others are good at it. But these actions must be interrupted, and a therapist can help evaluate a conflict that has already taken place, or one that comes up in therapy.

The Just Saying Fighters - These are the people who say, *"Don't take this the wrong way, but…"* or *"I'm sorry you took what I said to heart."* Ever frustrating, someone told them that it's acceptable to 'just say' what needs to be said, blurted out, at the expense of all diplomacy and emotional impact. While I'm a fan of using your words, using them in a way that puts yourself first as the *Public Service Announcement Champion* is not good for your relationships. And, it's less likely others will move to a feeling of safety and intimacy with you. Safety and intimacy are required for good communication, sexual connection and the pure joy of living.

The Love Tester - Testing the love involves setting others up to see if they will do what we want them to do by creating a scenario or dilemma to which they have to respond. To a trained therapist, love testing is obvious; but within a relationship, it can be disguised as a genuine need that begs for a loving response, which turns into a pattern of co-dependence. Love testing takes so much work! But, it often feels safer to the tester than using actual words to request what is desired.

The Mad Scientist - This is a form of truly getting others to execute your communication "dirty work." This takes a lot of work to set up. Essentially, the Mad Scientist is the orchestrator of a dialogue between two persons: we'll call them Person A and Person B. Person A is the person to whom the Mad Scientist should really be speaking directly. Person B is a stand-in communicator, has typically displayed more courage in the fight, and is used as a surrogate. The surrogate is often chosen because of their influence over the intended audience (Person A). Sometimes, Person B is chosen simply so the Mad Scientist can opt-out.

The Dead Horse Jockeys - Have you ever heard the term, *"Stop beating a dead horse?"* That horse can't take you anywhere. There are communicators who not only beat the horse but try to ride it in hopes of going places. It's just not going to happen. Dead horse jockeys like to bring up the past. They enjoy the historical story of the past hurt. Many times there is genuine unforgiven hurt present, and confronting it can eliminate this behavior. However, just as often, the dead horse is beaten to deflect from the accountability the jockey has in the race.

REFLECTION/ACTION

There's a lot of information in this section that may be lifting the blinds in your darkened room to let the sunlight in right now. You may have identified some of these behaviors in yourself or in those around you. Take some time to reflect on these behaviors and whether you can safely confront any of them.

Perhaps you could have a quiet conversation by sharing this book or sections of it. If you perceive a lack of safety in doing so, follow your intuition and seek help from a professional to guide these conversations. This book is not a replacement for professional counseling, although I desire that it be a road sign pointing toward it where needed, like a rest stop on a high-speed highway.

_____

_____

_____

_____

First Aid Kits and Other Helpful Tools

Stay Safe Out There

To see the world, things dangerous to come to, to see behind walls, draw closer, to find each other, and to feel. That is the purpose of life.

The Secret Life of Walter Mitty (Stiller, 2013)

CHAPTER THIRTY-SEVEN

Emotional Vocabulary

It is possible that you or someone you communicate with was never exposed to a rich or diverse vocabulary for healthy emotional expression. Even those who experienced emotions were sometimes exposed to simplistic words like "pissed, sad, glad, mad, or happy" and not many more. Other times, they may have attempted to tell others how they felt only to be shut down or told to *"Stop crying,"* or *"Only speak when you're spoken to."* In either case, these people will often use phrases like, *"I don't know,"* or *"It's weird,"* indicating that they've stumbled across a hot thought of emotion and have no language ready to express it.

Feelings are the lifeblood of life itself. They tell us what we're thinking and explain our resulting behavior. They tell us when we're on the right track and the wrong track. Even before we choose the words, we feel the feelings in our heads, hearts, and stomachs. If we leave these feelings unexpressed, they can manifest themselves as dis-ease and even disease in the body. Even after we feel extreme emotion and calm down later, the events need contextual understanding and debriefing, or they will be destined to find a home in yet another conflict. They will keep seeking expression and understanding until they are understood. Wouldn't you rather find the right words to express your emotions?

REFLECTION/ACTION

There are dozens of feeling-type words available to us. Search the internet and you'll stumble upon list after list of "feeling words." In therapeutic practice, it's vital that I am in tune with what my clients are feeling and that I teach them to find more refined word choices to convey their feelings. When clients dismiss their emotions, it's important that I coach them on finding their voice and using clear descriptors to express them. If you or someone you know missed out on having a diverse feeling vocabulary modeled by the teachers in your lives, do your own research and choose the words that describe how you're feeling. You may need to talk to someone about the words once you find them, so they can be integrated into your expression and story. Stand-alone words may not be enough, and having a professional to help you convey the new learning to others would be a natural and normal next course of action.

SAY ... Something!

CHAPTER THIRTY-EIGHT

Healthy Boundaries

When you're on a hike in the woods, there are three main areas of preparation that are key to a successful trip: access to a map with a determined destination in mind, a review of upcoming weather, and a clear understanding of the boundaries of the immediate path. As for the last part, the map won't always make this clear. You need to assess the boundaries yourself up close and through frequent communication with your hiking partner. You need to keep yourself and your journey partner safe. You need to know whether moving from the path outside the boundary will result in a slide down a hill, a twisted ankle, or an unexpected animal encounter.

In human interaction, boundaries are just as important. Who gets access to your leisure time? Who gets to bring drama to you, if anyone? Who gets to bring problems to solve? What type of conversations do you involve yourself in? How do you engage in them (e.g.,via text, phone call, or email)? Do you have healthy boundaries?

Examples of unhealthy boundaries are when someone has a *Come-to-the-Queen* attitude. In order to interact with them, you must initiate all of the contact and give all of the effort. Another example is when we allow *Court Jesters* to enter into our presence with any kind of drama or type of time-wasting activity. Maybe you just have an entire *King's Court* group of people in your life who don't even see who you really are. But, you have something they need, so they stick around. Maybe it's resources, maybe it's just someone to pass the time with, and maybe it's someone to abuse.

REFLECTION/ACTION

Are you growing in your present state with your current boundaries? Are you enabling those around you to get by without making an effort in your direction or requiring that their behavior or energy, while in your presence, be of a certain quality or standard? It may be time to reflect upon who you want to spend time with, doing what, and for what reasons. If you're consciously choosing what you're doing, fantastic! If not, take some action to gently move away from those who hold you and your growth back and toward those who will stretch and grow you.

_____

_____

SAY ... Something!

CHAPTER THIRTY-NINE

Roles and Identity

Have you defined your roles and identity, both for yourself alone and within your relationships? Do others have clarity about who you are and which roles you wish to play? How do you know if others do know and understand? We can't easily define what communication looks like between us if it sits between two unknown quantities.

There was a time years ago when roles were more defined, or seemed to be. Some were happy about this and others weren't at all. Now more than ever, we have to define these from scratch in every new relationship and each scenario within the relationship. There should be no assumptions made when entering into a new relationship. Even previously defined relationships, where roles were once clear, can suddenly become very unclear as circumstances change. Therapists call these "changeability factors," and they know that only one small tweak in the environment or among the players in the scene is enough to shift roles and bring the need for more communication. This is so often underestimated.

REFLECTION/ACTION

If you're entering into something new, or have experienced changes in your current relationship dynamics, spend some time assessing the roles you and others play. Are others assuming you will continue doing what you've always done? Do your roles need changing? If so, how will this change impact those around you? Any change needs to be negotiated and not just rolled into by default. Change managed by default breeds resentment.

If you hear yourself saying, *"They don't seem to mind"* or *"It's fine, I don't mind,"* that may be true for a short time. The absence of open and articulated agreement will come up to bite you like a snake on the path. I can almost guarantee it. If you're not yet in a significant relationship, spend time writing down which roles you believe you would be comfortable with, understanding that when you find another to share life with, these roles will have to be revisited.

_____

_____

_____

_____

_____

_____

_____

_____

_____

_____

_____

_____

_____

_____

_____

SAY ... Something!

CHAPTER FORTY

Values Determine How You Read the Map

If I asked you to define your core values, would you be able to give me 5-7 words that represent who you are and what you stand for? They might be idea words or action words, but they should be words that describe your guiding principles in life. Mine include:

Intentionality - What do you want?

Clarity - What does it look like?

Curiosity - Are you interested in it?

Engagement - Are you dedicating yourself to it?

Growth - Are you growing and improving?

While there might be other things I believe in, or words I use to describe myself, these words are specially selected to convey to all I meet that my actions will be based on them, and my choices will be guided by them.

Core values determine what you take into consideration and what you rule out when communicating with others. Don't underestimate this. They are as strong as filters and triggers from childhood and past trauma. Even if you can't recite yours out loud right now, I guarantee you have lived and continue to live by them on a subconscious level. In fact, they probably govern how you show up and interact with the world in most areas of your life. They govern how you make choices, speak, and think; and the sooner you can bring these values into consciousness to verify them and communicate them to others, the happier and more self-assured you will be. You will also learn what more you want to learn in this life and how you'd like to continue to grow.

REFLECTION/ACTION

Just as there are feeling word lists on the internet, you'll also find many value word lists. Search and find a list or two and circle the twenty words that resonate most strongly with you. Go through your list a few times to see which of the twenty words are similar and could be eliminated for redundancy. Keep doing this until you're left with a list of 5-7 words that mean something to you and that you'd be happy to put on your wall at home as an art piece for all who visit you to see. You'll be astounded by how meaningful these words can become. Don't be afraid to change them throughout the course of your life as your priorities change.

_____

_____

_____

_____

_____

_____

_____

_____

_____

_____

_____

_____

_____

_____

_____

_____

_____

_____

_____

_____

_____

_____

_____

_____

SAY ... Something!

CHAPTER FORTY-ONE

Using Assumptions For Good, Not Evil

You know what they say about assuming, right? But, what if we could use the same undeniable power that assumptions have, which is to blind us to outside input, for the good of a situation or person instead of for the bad? What if you could have a blinding positive assumption about someone? If we've lived for any length of time in this world, we've seen how wrong negative assumptions can go. If we're honest, it's because we were convinced beyond any doubt. So, why can't the same power fuel a positive assumption and help determine a positive outcome? It can. It's just not as easy to do.

Often, we become habitual assumers. We've seen behavior happen, attempted in our best efforts to change it (or haven't tried at all), and seen no change. We assume we know or can predict the other's response based upon a few observations. We assign meaning to verbal and non-verbal responses, making assumptions about the intentions behind them. These assumed intentions may not actually exist at all.

When you find yourself rigidly loyal to your negative assumptions, and you feel you've tried many times to give room for change or confront it, I suggest there is likely something missing in the confrontation approach. Perhaps there is something lacking in the form of an opposite positive assumption that could, if present, change the outcome. If we have the insight into the need for change, that is a sign that we have the insight to make the change if given a path forward. And, if we have the insight, usually others in our world have it too on some level. There are times when others have neither the insight nor the desire to make things better, and I'll elaborate on this later in the book.

In conflict and even pre-conflict, we have an internal dialogue or argument happening in our mind where past conversations and attempts to make change replay. Or, perhaps totally imagined conversations play for the first time as if that is how they will unfold if attempted in reality. So, we walk away feeling defeated or angry in the middle of a fight, or before we even start. In walking away, we reinforce our belief that conflicts cannot be resolved, making it more challenging for the next round. The resulting emotions from the imagined defeat have to go somewhere and usually embody other unhelpful actions and behaviors.

In giving up, we begin to engage in quid pro quo transactions or new actions based upon earlier assumptions. *"If you're going to do that, then I'll do this! That will teach you."* But, do these actions ever teach anyone a lesson? No, they don't. They may deprive, hurt, and inflame, but they certainly don't teach. Emotion, either positive or negative, is energy that must find a home in the most efficient way possible, so help it find a good home.

REFLECTION/ACTION

Today, start to make new assumptions about someone with whom you struggle to communicate effectively. Take some time to write down your beliefs, thoughts, feelings, and assumptions about them. Now, draw from those assumptions a few honest, reflective statements about what you expect to happen as a result. Then write down a "what if" statement that represents an opposite positive assumption for each negative assumption. What are the corresponding behaviors that might result from these positive assumptions?

_____

_____

_____

_____

_____

_____

_____

_____

_____

_____

_____

_____

_____

_____

_____

_____

_____

CHAPTER FORTY-TWO

Accountability and Follow-Up

One of the most important tools for your journey is accountability and follow-up. After conflict occurs (or to stop it from happening in the future), you and your communication partner need to plan a checkpoint for follow-up. It's likely that more than one checkpoint will be needed.

Instead, the alternative is far too common. We lie in wait to pounce on the next infraction or any sign of proof that someone wasn't listening to our requests. This, in a romantic relationship, can quickly lead to thoughts that you're not truly loved by the other. Yes, it is often that dramatic in the counseling process. To be fair, these thoughts feel very real at that moment. Feelings are truly driving negative beliefs and determining sequences of events. It's no different in the workplace, really. We do the same with our employers and employees and co-workers.

In a continuous effort to grow, let's avoid that alternative. Given that the issue has been discussed and assurances of improvement have been made, I suggest agreeing to your own form of accountability. We generally resist formalizing these accountability moments, but their success resides in their pre-planned nature.

REFLECTION/ACTION

Setting up true and regular accountability takes effort. No one really loves it, but it *is* necessary. Discuss what is reasonable between you and the person with whom you're communicating. Discuss what these accountability conversations should look like and how they will be done. Details matter and should be agreed beforehand, including the time and place. I often suggest getting out of the house; take a walk, go fishing, have a picnic, go to dinner. Do something that allows you to relax, talk, and be open to feedback. Talk about how things are going and whether any further improvements can be made toward the ideal outcomes.

_____

_____

_____

_____

CHAPTER FORTY-THREE

Taking Responsibility

The complement to setting up accountability practices is, of course, taking responsibility when you receive feedback as part of the process. Don't wait until the walk, or the meeting, or the picnic, or the dinner to do this. Do this on an active moment-by-moment basis. Catch yourself before others can, and be proactive in your awareness of what's happening as you interact with others. Examples of actions opposing accountability are deflection, defensiveness, and blaming. It takes far fewer words to just say, "That was me, my fault, I'm sorry." Going further to say, "It wasn't intentional," will help if that's the truth; but if it isn't, don't waste your breath on that deception. It's futile and will only dig you a deeper hole to crawl into. If you're going to say it wasn't intentional, make your actual intentions clear.

I find it disappointing that taking responsibility is becoming more rare as time passes, almost a lost art. When I see a child taking responsibility, I actively look around for their parents to see what rare beings raised such a child. If I observe a little longer, I inevitably witness other samples of assertive interchanges, glimpses of modeled critical thinking and open dialogue related to the development of a healthy and diverse feeling vocabulary. It all goes hand in hand.

REFLECTION/ACTION

The next time you see the first glimpse of conflict arising, run a few steps ahead and be a lookout, so to speak. Look for how you can feel and see the transgression before it is verbalized. In the act of seeing ahead, take early accountability for any of your actions that contributed to the situation, even if you had no intention to do so. You'll be amazed at how quickly you can de-escalate the situation. Enjoy the freedom and empowerment it gives you and others.

_____

_____

_____

_____

_____

_____

CHAPTER FORTY-FOUR

Curious Questions

Communication comes in layers, hidden in defense and fear of doing harm. Or, perhaps communication comes guns blazing and ready to injure. Either way, unless you're dealing with a full-blown personality disorder (more about that later), most people don't want to hurt you with their words. You will only benefit from helping them say what they need to say safely. People tell me that their words often become watered down or completely absent at the point in which they fear they may hurt someone. When we fear the capacity of others to hear an honest question or a piece of truthful feedback, allowing it to shut our mouths, there is no true relationship. This bears repeating: without complete openness and freedom to ask anything, out of genuine curiosity and loving interest (not necessarily romantic), there can only be exchanges that sound like a relationship but come nowhere near being authentic, trusted, and assertive communication within a relationship.

On the flip side, how many times has someone asked you a question, and you responded with the quickest answer you could think of? Perhaps you missed the question altogether. Instead, what if you asked them, *"What makes you ask that question?"* If you're not sure what you're even responding to, there's a high likelihood you will have not 'heard' them and an even higher likelihood that they will not 'hear' you when you respond. So many conflicts arise out of half listening and half answering. After a few back and forth volleys, we're suddenly in a full-blown battle.

It should be said that there are questions disguised as curiosity. Questions such as, *"What are you doing?"* as you're watching someone do something in a way that differs from yours. An alternative is, *"Would you do this please?"* or *"I'd prefer it if it was done this way, please."* Asking someone what they are doing is often followed by *"What do you mean, what am I doing?"* or *"What is that supposed to mean?"* Faced with a response like this, the conversation can quickly go downhill.

REFLECTION/ACTION

Why do we lose our curiosity? Perhaps we are genuinely losing interest. Perhaps we fear that asking too many questions is rude or will offend. Or, maybe it's just easier to criticize than genuinely ask questions. The issues of life are exacerbated by a lack of curiosity combined with negative assumption making, and they hide like a crouching tiger between the actual words spoken, just waiting to pounce into a full-blown conflict or conversation. We spend so much energy not saying what we need to say that it becomes a very foreign concept over time to be curious about each other.

What if you tried *"What makes me curious about you is..."* or *"I need help understanding something."* In doing this, a genuine tone of curiosity comes across rather than a potential intrusive tone of voice that conveys a power play. Trust the intimacy of the conversation. Be curious and trust that being both present and curious will have an impact and encourage reflection in the other person.

_____

_____

_____

_____

_____

_____

_____

SAY ... Something!

CHAPTER FORTY-FIVE

Share Your Dreams and Vision

What do you dream of? I'm not talking about the nightmare you had last night after you ate that spicy meal. I mean, what do you really dream of being, doing, having, and achieving? You are God's highest form of creation, gifted with the ability to vision, dream, and imagine yourself into your future state. So what does that look like? How are you using the gift of your imagination? Have you ever written down your dreams in graphic, beautiful detail? Have you attached dates to your dreams? Or, have you fallen into the habit of settling for the appearance of reality around you?

Here's a tougher question: Have you shared your dreams with anyone? This could be a best friend or life partner. If you are still seeking that partner, how prepared are you to speak your dream to them with boldness? Are you ready to claim it in their presence, and to know in your heart of hearts that anyone worthy of you will say *"Yes!"* and do whatever it takes to help you get there.

REFLECTION/ACTION

Spend an evening writing down your desires; and start with your wants. Trace the wants back to the associated goals required to get there. Link those goals to the theme of purpose running through them. The bigger, the better. The more impossible, the better. Who said you couldn't? No one has authority over your life to tell you what you cannot be, do, have, or achieve.

If you have a partner, whether in business or life, ask them to do the same. Once they have done the exercise, order in some good food and have a sharing session where you each share your dream goals. Light each other up! Tell each other your visions for each other, too. Then, talk about logistics and what resources you might need to see your dreams come to pass. Pray, talk, dream, and agree that there is more of life to be lived!

_____

_____

_____

_____

_____

CHAPTER FORTY-SIX

What Does It Look Like?

"What does that look like?" If I had $100 for every time I asked clients this question in therapeutic sessions and received a blank stare, or a *"that's a good question"* response in return, I'd be a millionaire. Details matter! We are habitually vague in our communication. Notice I didn't say intentionally vague, but *habitually* vague. We speak in concepts and often in reference to visual pictures in our own minds, but we don't always clue people in on the details of the picture. Many times we don't know what's in that picture beyond vague shapes and colors, and a rough idea of who is present.

As an example, clients may say to me… *"I just want him to show me he loves me."* I respond with, *"Great, and what does that look like for you?"* Not only do we need to know what it looks like, but we need to know what it actually means in terms of actions, frequencies of actions, tones of voices, types of touch, environmental surroundings, and the list goes on and on. We have not demanded clarity from ourselves in most instances, much less do we give that clarity to others. Yet, we are prepared to begrudgingly blame others for not presenting us with what we need, day after day, allowing resentments to build; and disconnection and transactionalism to set in.

Other examples are, *"I just want others to see we're on the same team,"* or *"I need to know you're in my corner,"* or *"I want to know that you believe in me and have my back."* These are all wonderful sentiments straight out of the movies, but what do they mean, and what do they actually look like? Do you realize that it's possible to have a 20+-year-old cold war over vague mental pictures? How sad is this? How empty?

Ultimately when I start to ask clarifying questions as if I'm the person who is being asked to respond to the request for change, not only am I modeling how to ask for clarification, but I'm helping to break it down to a level where the person receiving the new clarity can make an active choice about whether they can change those things. Alternatively, if the receiving person does not feel that they can do the things being asked of them, I show them how to further negotiate by offering what they *can* do. We just need to use the right words to get to the bottom of what the request looks like.

REFLECTION/ACTION

If you have a notion of something you wish was different in your relationships at home or work, have you provided enough clarity? If not, take some time to journal more detail around some of the aspects of the change you'd like to see.

Invite your co-communicators to do the same. If you're stuck, use the Magic Wand Question, which asks, *"If you woke up tomorrow and everything in your life was as it should be, without limitation, what would you be experiencing, seeing, and doing in your world?"* By taking each other into the visual space, the pictures will tell you everything you need to know. But, having received that initial information, don't stop there. Ask more questions about the picture in high living color detail, and then communicate to each other what you'd truly love to do to help each other get what you want.

_____

_____

_____

_____

_____

_____

_____

_____

_____

_____

_____

_____

_____

_____

_____

_____

_____

_____

_____

SAY ... Something!

CHAPTER FORTY-SEVEN

The Right Person, Thing, and Time

In an earlier chapter, I mentioned triangulation (seeking reinforcement from a third party) as an unhelpful activity in communication or within a relationship. The healthy opposite of this is to always approach the right person with the info, the confrontation, or communication needed. In other words, when you have something to say, go to the right person for the right thing, at the right time.

The right person is the person who can give you the most clarity if you have questions, or the most forgiveness if you need grace, and the most truthful reflection if that's what you seek. The right thing means you're only talking about things relevant to that person, with that person. In other words, you're not talking about other people in a negative way. The right time means you don't delay in getting your questions answered or your truth spoken. Yes, you choose the right time given the convenience of others and the best environment for receptivity. However, you'll want to avoid excessive delay, as it can lead to decay, entropy, wheels falling off the bus, and long periods of senselessly wasted funk, which is a fertile ground for negative assumptions and catastrophic thinking. Get out of your head and talk to each other.

REFLECTION/ACTION

What do you have on your mind or heart that needs to be addressed? Why haven't you addressed it? What scares you about addressing it? What is the worst that could happen? If you need help, does that help need to be professional help, or can you simply script it out and read it aloud to the person with whom you need to communicate? I'm not a fan of electronic communication such as email and text, but I do believe there is value in scripting out what you need to say. Just please, read it to the person in their presence where you can energetically connect. The only caveat is that you've assessed the safety in doing this. If you are in any kind of abusive situation, either psychologically or physically, this is not something I'd advise without professional help and/or legal advice. This goes for every piece of advice in this book. Safety first.

_____

_____

_____

_____

_____

_____

_____

_____

_____

_____

_____

_____

_____

_____

_____

SAY ... Something!

CHAPTER FORTY-EIGHT

Put the Pain Where the Pain Belongs

Are you trying to get someone to do something they don't want to do? Maybe you feel they should want to do what you're asking them, so you start with efforts to get them to want to do it on their own without any complaining, pleading, or nagging from you? We have two reasons for doing anything. Either it brings us pleasure, or we will do it to avoid feeling pain. Pleasure is in the eye of the beholder. You cannot convince anyone to be pleased or feel pleasure from anything they don't naturally feel. So, cross *that* off your list. People generally do what they want to do to make themselves happy on the pleasure front.

On the other hand, you do have somewhat of a say as to where pain points reside. You may not ever want to be the cause of someone's pain. No one wants to be. But, you can stop being the carrier of someone's pain points. You can stop being the shock absorber for their pain. I need to be clear about what I mean by pain. I don't mean pain from grief or loss where you feel compelled to bring comfort to loved ones when they need it. When I speak of pain here, I speak of the discomfort that comes with not doing what someone should be doing. The discomfort from accountability that moves someone from inaction to action is designed to do exactly that... to *move* them. If you become a stopper for that compelled action, you become a co-creator of dysfunction.

So often in the normal course of life events, we or our loved ones suffer emotionally from the bumps and obstacles on the road. It's important to shift into those moments quickly to provide temporary relief and transitional support. But when those moments turn into months and then years, we can and do sometimes lose our way. We reason that those who have "been through" what they've been through, "can't help" how they are now because of all they've been through. Even without traumatic experiences to hang this on, we can often assign them excuses of having a certain personality type or temperament that causes them to act a certain way. In doing this, we allow them to be inactive, unengaged, and not make efforts for themselves and others.

REFLECTION/ACTION

If you want things to change, you'll have to consider putting the pain where the pain belongs. If you've given up on asking someone to do something difficult for you or differently from how they do now, and you've made excuses as to why you believe it's just too hard for them to do it, consider putting the pain where the pain belongs. This might mean changing your behavior to stop doing things that remove the natural consequences of their actions. It may mean implementing a consequence for their behavior that you've never enforced.

I don't advocate for surprise attacking others with sudden unexpected pain or punishment; far from it. I'm talking about committing to your desires and the follow-through needed to reach them. In the chapter on assertive confrontation, I'll talk more about this. Keep reading.

_____

_____

_____

_____

_____

_____

_____

_____

_____

_____

_____

_____

_____

_____

_____

_____

_____

_____

_____

SAY ... Something!

CHAPTER FORTY-NINE

Making Witnessed Audible Choices

"Then, what did they say?" I've asked this question a number of times when working with clients and team members whom I lead. They begin by relaying the detailed play-by-play of a confrontation they were in, where they came away feeling confused about why it didn't go well. Perhaps they believe they did well in the confrontation, having had the courage to say something, but it didn't result in a permanent behavioral change. So now, they need guidance for the next round. The reason I am always curious to know what the verbal response was to a given confrontation or question is that it matters 100% of the time what the audible verbal response was or was not.

So many times, we confront or ask curious questions and then settle for silence or a very inadequate, *"I don't know"* as a response. Silence is not tacit agreement, contrary to what some may tell you. Silence without some type of audible *"yes"* or a detailed response that either validates what you've asked, or requests more information about it, can be assumed to be tacit disagreement or disengagement at best. So, when clients come into sessions and tell me a story about a conversation they've had and how proud they are that they asked a tough question or confronted a tough topic, I say *"Well done"* and then I ask them… *"and, then what did they say?"* When I crawl inside the conversation and get in between the words and the interplay of the dialogue, I can quickly discern who is avoiding what, either unintentionally or on purpose, and who is passively settling for half-baked responses. This, in essence, is the goal we all have. We must figure out who surrenders to the vague response. We must figure out how to ask better questions and require audible responses if we want true intimacy, honesty, and resolution to the issues of life. Someone always surrenders too early. Someone needs to lead you both back to the adventure trail for more conversation.

REFLECTION/ACTION

All conversations of a truly connected nature involve curious questions, clarity finding, journeying together toward accountability, calling each other out of hiding toward growth, and choice making. What I propose is that a true choice is only true when it's made with an audible voice in words that confirm some level of reflection, resolute acceptance, or position on the issue; and, if needed, makes demands for further clarification. Ultimately, choice-making involves a clear "yes" or "no." So, think through what questions you haven't been able to ask or just haven't tried to ask directly. What is it you'd like to know? Why don't you ask it in a way that expects a clear yes or no? The reality is, sometimes we're scared to know, and that's okay. Avoidance of learning the truth can creep up gradually into every relationship at some point. Be brave.

_____

_____

_____

_____

_____

_____

_____

_____

SAY ... Something!

CHAPTER FIFTY

Do the Math

If you struggle with asking direct or difficult questions, another way to seek new information is to use a *pain scale* to assess where someone's beliefs or thoughts lie. Medical practitioners use pain scales for a reason: numbers don't lie. An example might be, *"On a scale of 1-10, with ten being I'll never leave my job, how much do you enjoy your job?"* If I were to alternatively ask, *"Do you enjoy your job?"* I might get a response like, *"Yes,"* or *"Yeah it's fine."* Or, I might get a story about how stressful it is or how my boss is a pain in my neck. But, I won't get a true reading on satisfaction, nor will I get any information on what would make it a ten. I think you get the idea.

Another area in which we don't do the math is when we personally avoid accountability or when our scorekeeping is off. We tend to minimize the number of genuine attempts we and others make to bring about change. It is just easier to not keep track. We equate a lack of change with a lack of demonstrated love, and so to cope with the rejection of that, we minimize it. Do the math, keep a journal. While love does not keep a record of wrongs in the romantic story books (or even in the Biblical definition of love), it sometimes needs to keep a record of efforts to make things right, so that true loving confrontation and accountable connection can continue. It will help you know when things are actually getting better.

REFLECTION/ACTION

If it helps, when using a numeric scale, make the scale 1-5 with 5 being high, so there aren't so many numbers to choose from. This is especially useful if you're communicating with someone who is a slower, more contemplative decision-maker. Be sure to describe what a 1 represents and what a 5 represents, so that the number given in response makes more contextual sense. Ask the same question again down the road after changes have been made so you can see the progress. This all takes conscious engagement, intimacy, and risk of vulnerability, but wouldn't you rather be engaged in something that's alive, than spending years on the couch binge-watching TV while your life drifts by? It's your choice!

_____

_____

SAY ... Something!

CHAPTER FIFTY-ONE

The Four Keys to Assertive Confrontation

No one can argue with your experience. They can argue with an accusation you make about them, but they can't argue with your experience of them. I'm a huge fan of speaking from your own experience with curiosity so that you can engage others in helping you understand them better. *"But, I hate confrontation,"* you say. Most probably, what you hate isn't the confrontation done well, but the confrontation that goes south in the first few sentences because it comes out like a police interrogation, character assassination, or a comparison to your mother! Yes, I'd hate that too.

What we really need to remember, other than a tone of loving curiosity, are the four keys to a genuine confrontation. I alluded to these earlier in Chapter 33 when discussing assertiveness. Confrontation can be much more straightforward when you use the DESC script in the foundational work by Bower and Bower (2004). DESC stands for Describe, Express, Specify and Consequences. When using this script, try first writing down what you will say, and then practice saying it before you talk to the person.

DESCRIBE - We need to describe the situation or behavior as we experienced it, as completely and objectively as possible, sticking to the facts. Less is more here. Long drawn out stories are not helpful and can confuse the listener.

"What I experienced yesterday was that I cleaned the house all day by myself."

EXPLAIN - Express your feelings or thoughts about the behavior/situation. Try phrasing your statements using "I" and not "You." Beginning sentences with "you" often puts people on the defensive, which means they are less willing to listen to you. Yes, you'll need to have a vocabulary of feeling words as discussed in Chapter 37. Without sharing the emotional impact, we cannot expect to obtain empathy from the person we're confronting. Most of the time, others have no idea that there's been an emotional event at all unless we clue them in.

"I felt overwhelmed, exhausted and frustrated."

SPECIFY - (I also sometimes call this SUGGESTING the alternative). Specify or suggest what behavior/outcome you would prefer to happen next time. Letting others know how they could do better as quickly as possible, and giving them the opportunity to choose to do or not to do it is vital. You would want them to do that for you.

"I would like us to work together on cleaning, dividing the work. This way, we'll be done in half the time, and can enjoy relaxing afterward."

CONSEQUENCES - Verbalize the intended and unintended consequences if this happens, both positive and negative. This isn't a threat of retaliation but is the raising of awareness of what will happen if an unattended emotional event doesn't get rectified.

"If I have to clean alone, without help, I will be too tired to go out afterwards or too tired to enjoy our friends when they come over to visit and I will build up resentment because I didn't get help."

REFLECTION/ACTION

Think of something that has recently happened causing an unwanted emotional state, perhaps prompting you to escalate and fight, or retreat and give in. No doubt, if you escalated the situation, you probably regret it now. Also, without any doubt, if you retreated and withdrew, it's still eating at you. Script out this four-component confrontation in your own words, and review it to remove any unnecessary words. Each component only needs one or two sentences. Anything more is unnecessary and is a veer off the path. Once you have something ready to share, ask if you can sit down with the person and read it to them. If needed, let them know you're reading it aloud because you struggle to naturally bring it up. Alternatively and ideally, memorize your statement and practice it so that you can convey it without reading it. Either way, ask for an opportunity to speak and share. You will see how powerful this can be if done with all four keys and with a loving energy of mutually beneficial solutions for the relationship.

_____

_____

_____

_____

_____

_____

_____

_____

_____

_____

CHAPTER FIFTY-TWO

Safe Responses to Hot Topics

The good news is, as you attempt to implement some of the suggestions in these pages, your own awareness of the part you have played in miscommunication and misunderstanding will increase rapidly. As it increases, you will catch yourself more quickly, and you'll find that you can implement an increasing number of safe responses to hot topics. Some examples of safe responses might include:

Tell me more about that...

Let me check if I understand...

Help me understand because I'm curious about...

That's interesting. I never thought of it that way...

Let me take another shot at saying that differently...

I see it differently, but I appreciate your perspective...

I'm just a little tired right now. Do you mind if I rest and we discuss it at (time)?

I'm overwhelmed emotionally right now. Let me calm down so I can find words...

We are sometimes challenged to find these words before the emotional overwhelm sets in, but in a healthy, assertive relationship, it's our mission to manage the risk of overwhelm and find words no matter what feelings are occurring.

REFLECTION/ACTION

Choose your favorite two phrases from the list above, or create your own variations that sound more authentic to your normal way of speaking. Go to someone you care about or live with and let them know that you plan to practice using these phrases next time you're tired and overwhelmed, or next time you would have normally just responded with a "yeah" or an "uh-huh" without really listening. Ask for some accountability and some grace to go with it, in case it comes out a little clumsily at first. Don't be afraid to commit, and don't be afraid to take some feedback if you don't quite get it right the first few times.

_____

_____

_____

_____

CHAPTER FIFTY-THREE

Seek First to Understand

Stephen Covey said it best: "Seek first to understand." (Covey, 2004, p.235). Often, we listen with the intent of responding, instead of listening to really *listen* and learn more. If you truly seek first to understand before being understood, you will put curious questions first, and put the needs of others before your own. You will let others finish speaking before you respond. When you respond, you will respond in a way that is seeking more information. Seeking first to understand is essentially a decision you make and a position you stand for. It's a principle of communication that gives before it seeks to get.

REFLECTION/ACTION

How can you implement this in your world? The first step is to claim it as a decision you're making, and to do so with witnesses who can hold you accountable for your decision. Then, it can be as simple as staying focused on the other person as they speak, asking more questions to gain clarity, and ending with, "Is there more I need to understand?" They will tell you, if you sincerely ask.

_____

_____

_____

_____

_____

_____

_____

_____

_____

CHAPTER FIFTY-FOUR

Never Use Never or Always

This is key. When we're communicating with others, and especially when we're emotionally invested, we all have a tendency to say things like, *"You never take out the trash"* or *"You always interrupt me."* We all have a tendency to abuse these two words at times. It's very frustrating to be the recipient of an *always* or *never* statement, and it feels like there's no safe road back from an accusation like that. Imagine that you've been pushed off a cliff, hanging on with a few fingers, fighting for your life. Why would you want to inspire that kind of helpless feeling in someone you care about? If you wouldn't want it done to you, don't do it. This is a short chapter, because it's just that simple.

REFLECTION/ACTION

Honestly assess whether you're using the words, always or never in your conversations. Change your approach to a healthy assertive confrontation discussed earlier. Even if a transgression has happened dozens, or even hundreds of times, it's not always, and it's unlikely that the thing you find lacking has never ever happened.

_____

_____

_____

_____

_____

_____

_____

_____

_____

SAY ... Something!

When Nothing Is Working

Calling for Help, Sending up Flares, and Getting Located

Help will always be given at Hogwarts, Harry, to those who ask for it.

Harry Potter and the Deathly Hallows - Part 2 (Yates, 2011).

CHAPTER FIFTY-FIVE

Is That The Time?

So, how do you know when you're in the wrong conversations or maybe even the wrong relationships? The only thing worse than not being heard is being heard and then having nothing acted upon by others. What do you do if you've read the books, tried the things, and nothing is working? It takes two to tango, or at least you and someone else have to both show up for a conversation to take place. What if all your effort isn't reciprocated? What if you've tried, and they just won't say something back?

When you've reflected, analyzed, taken action, and asked for action in return and it isn't reciprocated, you may need to make some choices to move on toward healthier conversations elsewhere. But, before you do, seek professional help in the form of a Licensed Marriage and Family Therapist (LMFT) or Family Systems Educated Counsellor. Gottman Relationship Therapy skills are also very helpful in a therapist's toolkit. Its founders, John M. Gottman PhD. and Julie Swartz Gottman PhD. (The Gottman

Institute, 2021), have spent years researching, practicing, and informing evidence-based practice to help people improve communication and identify when the end of a relationship might be near and why.

At the end of the day, we all have choices. You can't make someone else change. You can only present yourself as a willing participant in the desired change and ask for the dance from a willing partner. When they desire to change, they will. Most importantly, you deserve having someone show up for you. Don't settle for less.

REFLECTION/ACTION

If you're in this position and need to seek professional advice, do your research. It's always recommended that you ask for testimonials. Make sure, before you agree to a therapeutic relationship, you discuss all the same terms of engagement you seek from a relationship partner. Discuss with the therapist how everyone involved will give and receive healthy feedback in the therapeutic process. Ask them what their process is generally, and which tools they use. Inquire about their strengths and skills as a therapist, and help them understand what it is you are looking for. A quality therapist will make sure they are equipped with the skills and tools you need before they embark on the journey with you. An ethical therapist will have a clear way of keeping healthy boundaries with you and your communication partners while they seek to help you all. They should also be open and honest with you if they perceive that they do not have those skills in your particular situation. Ask questions until your mind and heart both say "yes."

_____

_____

_____

_____

_____

_____

_____

_____

_____

_____

SAY ... Something!

CHAPTER FIFTY-SIX

Abusers, Sabotagers, and Clinical Diagnoses

There are times when we allow the noisy, unreasonable, and even unstable people to win while we shut down. Even worse, we may run away from something we worked hard to build before they arrived on the scene, surrendering it all to them in an effort to find peace. There are times we are worn down by abusers of various kinds. In workplace environments, as in personal relationships, we sometimes find entire work teams working to the lowest common denominator of the most demanding team member in the room as they tiptoe around them, not confronting, for fear of escalating erratic behavior. We tend to do what is least painful at any given moment. Remember we generally seek pleasure and avoid pain.

Whether at home or at work, the tendency is to read an online quiz definition of narcissism or some other personality disorder and start diagnosing those around us. I think someone once invented a term for this as *"being an armchair psychologist."* Friends, this is so dangerous. Making a clinical diagnosis is serious business. It calls for the help of a trained clinical therapist to both diagnose and create a treatment plan for the diagnosed individual, with their full consent. Treatment plans make sure progress is made and goals are regularly assessed throughout the therapeutic journey.

REFLECTION/ACTION

If you or someone close to you suspects a diagnosis should be made, please don't do this at home. Seek the help of a knowledgeable professional who is trained in the use of today's accepted diagnostic tools, as these change over time. Then, ensure that beyond diagnosis they know how to help you and have had exposure to working with that diagnostic label for some time and with success. This will involve being brave enough to ask for success stories when perhaps you're feeling too vulnerable to do so. Take your time, breathe. The circumstances you seek resolution for weren't built in a day, so the solution is unlikely to be either.

_____

_____

_____

_____

Beyond Hindsight

Principles for the Journey

King Arthur: "God uses people
like you, Lancelot. Because your heart
is open. You hold nothing back.
You give all of yourself."

Lancelot: "If you knew me better,
you would not say such things."

King Arthur: "Oh, hey, I take the
good with the bad, together.
I can't love people in slices."

First Knight (Zucker, 1995)

CHAPTER FIFTY-SEVEN

Principle-Centered Adventuring

Principle #1 - You Are a Walking, Talking Polarity

Stop your all-or-nothing thinking. People aren't all good or all bad. We are all walking, talking polarities. And, like King Arthur, you shouldn't love people in slices. We have infinite potential for good and are all vulnerable to acting beneath our stated and desired standards. It's all part of the human condition. Go into your adventure knowing that you and your journey partner will not be perfect, and you will not always do as you say you will do after the day you make all the lovely promises to each other. In every so-called *bad* situation, look for the equal and opposite *good*. For every diversion from the path, look for the growth opportunity. As long as you both keep showing up to the conversation, go in peace, knowing that's all there is.

Principle #2 - Where There Is No Vision, There Is No Need for a Map

This should be obvious. But, without vision there isn't a mountain to climb, a river to cross, nor a hike to take. So many relationships and life adventures start with a vision, but through the course of normal life events and happenings, the vision becomes blurry or takes the backseat for other critical priorities at the time. You must pull it back off the shelf and dust it off, even when you think it isn't dusty. If it hasn't been discussed in over a year, it's dusty. Take it down and talk about it. If you avoid re-evaluating your visions and navigating your map, you'll find yourself lost.

Principle #3 - Goals Are Your North Star

Just as with vision, goals are vital for setting and staying on course. Milestone goals and bigger impossible dream goals to help you create together, adventure together, and serve your wider community are all part of what will make your adventure meaningful, efficient, and effective. There is no better way to feel accomplished and to stay focused on the right things than to know your goals and where you're headed together. Without this, automatic habits will chart your course by default.

Principle #4 - Your Self-Image Is Your Compass

Before, during, and after your journey with someone else, you must have a clear self-image to support your vision and goals. If you can't see yourself doing what you want to do, you must change your self-image until you see it and believe it. Self-image isn't selfishness. It is, in essence, developing your own character according to your core values and what you admire in others. It is scripting a movie in which you identify yourself as the leading character first, so you can easily determine who the supporting cast must be. Of course, once this is defined, there is expected interplay between characters, and a delightful and fulfilling story will inevitably unfold. And, sometimes successive seasons need to bring new character development. That is to be expected. Like vision, bring it down from the shelf and dust it off often.

Principle #5 - Continuous Improvement Over Delayed Perfection

No one ever arrives at their destination. There are successive destinations in your journey, each with its own challenges and opportunities to express your purpose. Each destination requires stretching and growing in order to reach it. If you sit at home planning your journey out until you think it's perfect, you may never go. Understand that in setting out, you have agreed to a life of continuous improvement. Plan, but acknowledge that you will have to make adjustments as you go through acts of self-improvement, environmental changes, higher vision, higher purpose, and even sometimes changed values from the impacts of the road you've traveled. Life changes us and it should. Get moving!

Principle #6 - Gratitude Magnetizes

Practice gratitude, every single moment of every single day. Each morning and evening, think of five things you're grateful for. Why are you thankful for those things? Feel the feelings of gratitude deep down in your soul. Don't keep this to yourself. Share it verbally with others who can share the joy and emotion of your gratitude. Make sure your list includes people, places, and things. Thank your creator—whoever you conceive that to be—because they are on your journey with you, whether or not you acknowledge their presence. You, whether you are a co-creator in this world, with infinite possibilities to imagine, be, do and have a life more abundant than the one you may be experiencing at this moment. It's all yours; go get it!

Principle #7 - Affirmation Cultivates

When you're not feeling the gratitude, construct a positive affirmation about a desired future state and speak it aloud until you can connect to the feelings associated with that future state. *I'm so happy and grateful now that…* is an example of how to begin. Adjust the affirmation until your heart says yes to the words you've carefully chosen. Some believe affirmations are lies and therefore can't settle into utilizing them to change their beliefs or thoughts. Whether you agree with affirmations or don't, understand that your subconscious mind is an empty garden bed awaiting seed. Wouldn't you rather be an intentional planter of that seed, than a passive recipient of random seeds dropped by passing birds or carried on the breeze? It really is that simple. Once planted, the ideas that take hold are the thoughts that are regularly watered and sun-kissed (i.e., reviewed and restated daily). Your mind doesn't care what it grows, so be intentional about what you plant, and what you nurture and cultivate. This part is up to you. Continuous, repetitive affirmations with a firm belief in the value-based, purpose-filled outcome are necessary to keep you focused and intentional and seeking mutually beneficial milestones.

Principle #8 - Persistence Is Everything

Have you ever heard the phrase *"Start as you mean to go on?"* Of course, this is referring to the first steps of your journey being so intentional and so true to your values and vision that they get you to the end destination. But, successful journeys require persistence if those initial well-intended steps are to carry you further. Persistence is also key for the correcting of those steps when you're off track. Even if the first steps weren't great, your stride can be improved as you go, so long as you keep moving forward consciously.

_____

_____

_____

_____

_____

_____

_____

_____

_____

_____

_____

CHAPTER FIFTY-EIGHT

The Journey Ahead

This book is a labor of love. My desire when I conceived the idea was to write a book that was as close to the intimate conversation in a client session as it could be, but one that would reach a wider audience. As I write the final chapter, I'm chatting in instant messenger applications with clients who are actively encouraging me and thanking me for traveling on their journey with them. Some are writing their wedding vows for a wedding in a few days. Others are sharing happy pictures from their weekend. Some are happily married, and some are happily divorced, experiencing new love because of my work with them. What a blessing to do this work, and what a joy to see my fellow travelers as they journey and to be there for them when they need a fresh perspective.

I hope this book will help you, the reader I may never meet. That is my heart's desire. I thank God for giving me the opportunity to speak into your lives, the clients I will know personally, and the readers I have only dreamed of until now. And I thank God for all the many members of my work teams who follow me as well as the leaders I've followed, both past and present, including those I didn't think I was learning from at the time. You have made me a better leader. You have tested my communication theories and taught me what to keep and throw out, making me a better communicator. Rest assured, you are on these pages somewhere. With my whole heart, I wish you abundance, peace and the realization of your highest selves. Marleta.

THE END

END NOTES

SECTION ONE

Opening Page

- Fincher, D. (Director). (2008). *The curious case of Benjamin Button* [Film]. Paramount Pictures; Warner Bros. Pictures; The Kennedy/Marshall Company.

Chapter 2

- Cassavetes, N. (Director). (2004). *The notebook* [Film]. New Line Cinema.

Chapter 9

- *Holy Bible*, New Living Translation. (1996). Tyndale House Publishers, Inc.

SECTION TWO

Opening Page

- Strayed, C. (2012). *Wild: From lost to found on the Pacific Crest Trail*. Alfred A. Knopf

Chapter 15

- Covey, S. R. (2004). *The 7 habits of highly effective people: Powerful lessons in personal change* (15th ed.). Free Press.

Chapter 16

- Nightingale, E. (1966, 2018). *Lead the field.* Nightingale Conant Corporation. Sound Wisdom Publishing.

SECTION THREE
Opening Page

- Columbus, C. (Director). (1999). *Bicentennial man* [Film]. Touchstone Pictures; Columbia Pictures; 1492 Pictures; Laurence Mark Productions; Radiant Productions.

Chapter 29

- Chapman, G. D. (2015). *The five love languages: The secret to love that lasts.* Northfield Publishing.

Chapter 30

- Rousseau, D. M. (1995). *Psychological contracts in organizations: Understanding written and unwritten agreements.* Sage Publications.

SECTION FOUR
Opening Page

- Webb, M. (Director). (2014). *The amazing spider-man 2* [Film]. Columbia Pictures; Marvel Entertainment; Arad Productions, Inc.; Matt Tolmach Productions.

Chapter 33

- Bower, G. H. & Bower, S. A. (2004). *Asserting yourself: A practical guide for positive change.* (Updated Edition). Da Capo Lifelong Books.

SECTION FIVE

Opening Page

- Stiller, B. (Director). (2013). *The secret life of Walter Mitty* [Film]. Samuel Goldwyn Films; Red Hour Productions; New Line Cinema; TSG Entertainment; Big Screen Productions; Ingenious Media.

Chapter 51

- Bower, G. H. & Bower, S. A. (2004). *Asserting yourself: A practical guide for positive change.* (Updated Edition). Da Capo Lifelong Books.

Chapter 53

- Covey, S. R. (2004). *The 7 habits of highly effective people: Powerful lessons in personal change* (15th ed.). Free Press.

SECTION SIX

Opening Page

- Yates, D. (Director). (2011). *Harry Potter and the deathly hallows - part 2* [Film]. Warner Brothers Pictures; Hey Day Films.

Chapter 55

- The Gottman Institute: A research-based approach to relationships. (2021), https://www.gottman.com.

SECTION SEVEN

Opening Page

- Zucker, J. (Director). (1995). *First Knight* [Film]. Columbia Pictures; Zucker Brothers Entertainment.

ACKNOWLEDGMENTS

I'd like to thank my family and friends who have watched over me and cared for me while I've taken all the time I need to get this project done. And for all my muses, you know who you are. I'm grateful for having you all in my life and having a life where I can be myself and use my gifts to fully express my voice. There's a lot more coming. I love you all!

ABOUT THE AUTHOR

Marleta Black is a psychologist, writer, leader, thinker, musician, and an original introverted misfit (in no particular order of importance). Marleta uses her life-long passion for learning, lessons from overcoming her own communication challenges  and her unique way of synthesizing and distilling thoughts to provide crystallized moments of clarity for those she leads, coaches and counsels. Marleta is a communication and conflict resolution coach for businesses, their teams and extended families in Clearwater, Florida. She also works with couples in relationship counseling and with individuals experiencing life transitions and setting BIG goals for living their best life. Prior to residing in Clearwater, she lived in Australia for 30 years, becoming a dual citizen and raising a family of three thriving children with her husband Phil, conquering cultural differences and forging a fruitful career in Information Technology and Human Services.

Contact the author at MarletaBlackCoaching.com

Made in United States
Orlando, FL
02 November 2021

10158364R00142